# QUEEN, SPEAK OUT

Copyright © 2021 Christine H. Sandoval. *All Rights Reserved.*
Published by Christine H. Sandoval.

Front Cover design by Matt Davies
Layout design by Laura Jones

The purpose of copyright is to fuel creativity, encourage authors to produce original content, and promote free speech. Uploading or distributing photos, scans, or any content from this book without prior permission is theft of the author's intellectual property. Thank you for buying an authorized edition of this book and for complying with copyright laws.

For special orders, quantity sales, course adoptions, and corporate sales, please email the publisher at sales@drchristinesandoval.com.

Queen, Speak Out: *How to Rediscover Your Voice and Become Your Own Champion in Life and at Work*

First paperback edition: April 2021
ISBN 978-1-7368289-0-8 *Paperback*
978-1-7368289-1-5 *Ebook*

Printed in the United States of America

# QUEEN, SPEAK OUT

How to Rediscover Your Voice and
Become Your Own Champion in
Life and at Work

CHRISTINE H. SANDOVAL

For Mia

# CONTENTS

Introduction: Chaos on the Outside, Calm on the Inside     i

## PART ONE: DIG DEEP

Chapter 1: The Making of a Queen     3
Chapter 2: Your Self-Silencing Is Negatively Impacting Your Well-Being     19
Chapter 3: How Did You End Up Not Speaking Out for Yourself     35

## PART TWO: TRANSFORM FROM WITHIN

Chapter 4: You Can Choose to Free Your Voice     53
Chapter 5: Speaking Out and Self-Care     69
Chapter 6: Ten Steps to Get Good at Speaking Out for Yourself     87

## PART THREE: BE AS YOU ARE

Chapter 7: Find Your Own People     111
Chapter 8: Pick Your Battles to Get Smart About Speaking Out     125
Chapter 9: Grow Your Knowledge to Keep Speaking Out     139

Conclusion: Let's Hear You Roar, Queen     155

Acknowledgments     157
About the Author     159
Book Review     160

# INTRODUCTION

## Chaos on the Outside, Calm on the Inside

**YOU'VE BEEN DUPED.**

In the thick forest of the obsolete, the old, worldly kings held the keys to the kingdom. The gluttons, cowards, hypocrites, and the greedy conjured up lopsided rules: "All humans are created equal" became "All *men* are created equal." Women were relegated to be second-class citizens.

Kings insisted that Queens keep quiet and represent the epitome of grace, class, and dignity. Queens who spoke up were labeled as witches—beheaded and burned at the stake, figuratively and literally. Incentive structures made of adulation, acceptance, belonging, and physical protection were erected so the mirage that made women see themselves as inferior to men became a norm.

In actuality, the silencing of women maintained the status quo at the expense of their peace, joy, sanity, and health. Self-silencing is a wretched killer associated with depression, eating disorders, irritable bowel syndrome, and cardiovascular disease, to mention a few undesirable repercussions.

Nonetheless, as with any house made of cards and built on sand, the end of the patriarchal construct is at hand. Clowns are being caught. Deceit-dealers are being exposed. Lionesses are awakening to their true self and reigniting their roar. Many are making this vow: "Never again will my daughters, granddaughters, or I be silenced—not on my watch."

I see you, Queen.

Your head is down. Your breathing is fast and shallow. Your mind is racing with overwhelming to-dos and worries. Your heart is aching. Your pain is palpable. You feel invisible. Your dreams are on life support. You're tired.

You've kept mum to keep peace most of your life. Yet while an outsider sees your perfectly curated highlight reel, you are floundering inside. "But I've invested too much to speak out now" is what you tell yourself. So you let the sinking feeling of hiding your truth turn into criticism, defensiveness, contempt, and stonewalling. After all these years, it's now eroding your most significant relationships.

"Can this downward spiral end now?" you beg under your breath. Yes, it can. And it has to end in your lifetime so the Queens of future generations do not have to succumb to the agony you're enduring due to self-silencing.

How would it feel to have chaos on the outside while embodying calm on the inside?

Voicing out rattles your surroundings yet quiets your soul. Speaking out is like a torpedo blasting the world you've always known while creating a sanctuary in your spirit. Then wherever you go, you have a home. You always belong. You experience deep healing. If applicable, you may even go on a lower dose of medication, self-selected and prescribed.

Queen, it's time to pick up your crown and wear it proudly. You alone have the power to reset expectations on how others treat you. Your words are your lever and sword. You can be brave, strong, and feminine at the same time.

In this book, I'm going to show you, step-by-step, how you can rediscover your voice. Throughout the following chapters, you will be held and supported until speaking out becomes natural to you.

In the Filipino culture, in which I was born and raised, it isn't unusual for women to be the heads of the household. They typically support their husbands and children financially. Yet in the workplace, these same Queens were expected to check their crowns at the door and hold in their truth. "Keep your head down. Don't ask too many questions. Focus on your work." This was the cultural definition of an excellent work ethic. They would wait decades to be promoted, if at all. And they killed themselves at work only to come home depleted. Burnout was real.

Then I moved to the United States and moved up the ladder in corporate America. There I got to know a tiny fraction of men and women leaders who acquired huge influence in the organization while having vibrant close relationships and maintaining their vitality. Most of them spoke up for themselves firmly and with confidence.

I set out to study what it took to grow the inner strength that radiated throughout the rooms they inhabited. For thirteen years, I took copious notes as I interviewed, observed, and studied the mindset and habits of role models in corporate, business, academia, healthcare, and creative spaces. Then I applied the strategies and tactics in my life. They worked well. After tens of iterations, I refined and distilled the core essentials that formed my personal system. I taught many others in bite-sized pieces throughout my journey. But in this book, I lay the full lessons down.

While this book can serve as an ultimate guide to speaking out for yourself, it's not a silver bullet. Start here. Make progress. Then keep researching other tools to help you become a master self-advocate.

Knowing and accepting your identity as a Queen is where the journey begins. Let's ride.

# PART ONE:

## Dig Deep

# CHAPTER 1

## The Making of a Queen

**YOU WERE BORN A QUEEN.** What feelings does this statement generate when you read it? Do you immediately say to yourself, "Maybe other women were born a Queen, but not me."? I hear you. I see you.

When you think of a Queen, what images come to mind? Do you see a woman with porcelain skin tone, wavy hair, blue eyes, and straight teeth? How do you perceive her? Do you think of her as well-dressed, soft-spoken, eloquent, and composed? Do you have a few or none of these qualities? If your answer is yes to some or all of the above, then it's not surprising for you to feel wrong to think of yourself as a Queen. You're not alone.

What makes a woman a Queen, anyway?

A Queen, by definition, is the most powerful chess piece that each player has, able to move any number of unobstructed squares in any direction along a rank, file, or diagonal on which it stands. In contrast, a pawn is a chess piece of the smallest size and value. It can only move one square at a time.

Your life is akin to a game of chess, and you are its most powerful piece. If you acknowledge that you are the Queen of your life, then you move on the board of life as one. However, when you, the Queen, see yourself as a pawn, you'll limit yourself, minimizing your value to the smallest. You'll move one square at a time even when you have the capacity to move beyond.

How you see yourself determines whether you speak out for yourself or not. When you see yourself as a Queen, you realize there's power in your voice. Your voice has the power to build or destroy, heal or kill, mend or break, and free or take captives. You control that power.

Is there something in your life that needs building, healing, mending, or freeing? Your voice is key to deliver that need. Similarly, your voice can destroy, kill, break, or take captive those that no longer serve you.

When you embody your royal position and become aware that your voice carries your gifts, you make intentions and actions toward its expression. Having a voice becomes a norm. Silence becomes strategic. You flip the script from feeling intimidated in speaking your truth to becoming an inspiration for standing in your power.

## Choose to Accept or Reject Your Queenliness.

Now that you're aware of your character as Queen and its significance in shaping your life, the next step is accepting this identity. It takes one thing: your choice. You can make the decision right this moment to accept or reject your role as the Queen of your own life. When you embrace becoming a Queen, you sign up to take full ownership of where you are now, where you'll be heading, and how you'll live to get to your desired end point. You'll drop the reasons—valid or not—for not standing up for yourself. You'll begin the healing process of acknowledging your wounds from the past, seeking guidance and help to overcome, and pressing onward and upward when the going gets tough.

## Develop Tenacity to Keep on Keeping On.

When you decide to live as a Queen and begin to speak out for yourself, you're bound to encounter fresh challenges. Being tenacious is the skill that you'll need to go through the storm and get to the other side. On the other end of this journey, you'll feel confident in bringing your full self wherever you go.

Tenacity is often mislabeled as its negative sibling, stubbornness. If you've been told you're hard-headed, you have tenacity. You need to direct this force in ways that bring the best out of your circumstances and out of you. When it comes to speaking out, tenacity—the quality of being able to grip something firmly—is required. The road to rediscover your voice is tough, non-linear, and long.

If you're not naturally inclined to be tenacious, there's hope. Like many skills, tenacity can be learned and practiced.

**How to Develop the Tenacity to Speak Out for Yourself.**

1. Know and emotionally connect with your *why*.

Think of your why as the gravity or magnet within you that pulls you toward your goal. When problems arise or unexpected events happen, you're more likely to maintain focus when you're clear on why you do what you do. There'll be a number of distractions that may cause you to stop developing the ability to speak out for yourself. Your why will refocus you. It will bring you back on track.

Fill in the blank. I want to speak out because I want to start, stop, or continue to _____.

Reflect on the areas in your life where you tend to bite your tongue and hold your feelings in. Is it at work? With your partner? When discussing certain topics that trigger past traumas?

Make a note of why you want to speak out for yourself. Is it because you want to continue to set an example for your children on how to protect and stand up for themselves? Is it because you want to stop feeling unheard and unseen at work or in your important relationships? Is it because you want to start showing yourself and others that your voice matters?

Let's use the **Five Whys Technique** to get to the root of your desire.

> A. Why do you want to make speaking out a habit?
> B. For the answer in A, ask why?
> C. For the answer in B, ask why?
> D. For the answer in C, ask why?
> E. For the answer in D, ask why?

Your answer in E is your root why.

Here's an example.

> A. I want to make speaking out a habit because I feel trapped in life.
> B. I feel trapped in life because a voice inside of me is hidden.
> C. A voice inside of me is hidden because I value others' opinions over my own.
> D. I value others' opinions over my own because I was raised that way.
> E. I was raised that way because well-meaning people didn't know how to protect and uplift my self-esteem.

Thus, the example's root why is: "I want to make speaking out a habit because I want to protect and uplift my self-esteem."

Your why is your North Star. It's your reference point to keep you focused despite setbacks, chaos, and darkness. It's your firm hold of the future life you'll love.

Emotionally get connected to this why. What does this desire mean to you? Feel it in your gut. Let it sink into your heart. Want it as badly as you need to breathe.

**2. Feel and visualize the outcomes of *not* developing the tenacity to make speaking out a habit.**

The definition of insanity, according to the genius Albert Einstein, is "doing things the same way over and over and expecting a different result."

What could happen if you continue to hold back your voice for three more years?

- How would you feel about yourself?
- How would you feel about the person(s) you've been having opposing views with but didn't share your thoughts and feelings with them?
- What is your energy level? Would you feel more alive or more depressed?
- How would you rate your overall well-being and quality of life?

**3. Similar to Step #2, feel and visualize the outcomes of developing the tenacity to make speaking out a habit.**

What could happen if you stop holding back your voice and begin speaking out for yourself in the next three years?

- How would you feel about yourself?
- How would you feel about the person(s) you've been having opposing views and you shared your thoughts and feelings with them?
- What is your energy level? Would you feel more alive or more depressed?
- How would you rate your overall well-being and quality of life?

**4. Practice regularly. Start with low-stake risks and gradually take on heavier stuff.**

Only through consistent practice can we turn intentions into actions and actions into muscle memory.

As with most learning journeys, speaking out is not an overnight process. You have to keep showing up on a regular cadence whether you feel like doing it or not.

A way to build tenacity in practice is beginning to speak out on low-stake issues. For instance, when I was recovering from being with a possessive boyfriend for over a year, I didn't immediately regain the independent thinking and self-confidence that I had before the psychological manipulation.

In my teenage years, this boyfriend was protective and later became possessive. Initially, he would share with me how modesty in clothing represents an enviable inner character. Then, he moved on with buying me new clothes of his preferred style to replace my whole wardrobe. I ended up being shamed if I wore anything above the knee or a sleeveless top. As we got deeper into the relationship, he started refraining me from talking to my friends. He would repeatedly preclude me from talking to schoolmates, teachers, or anyone of the opposite gender. It got worse, and then the ultimatum came—he made me choose between our relationship and an internship of my dreams. Wisely, I chose the internship, which turned out to be a catalyst for my personal and professional growth.

Following the fallout of a toxic relationship, I began to rebuild my sense of self and rediscover my voice. I started with the seemingly small stuff like wearing above-the-knee shorts. Then, I wore sleeveless tops. Over the succeeding years of making choices and speaking out for myself, I regained my self-confidence. Years later, I made being with someone who is self-assured and appreciative of who I am a non-negotiable for dating and relationships.

**5. Do daily affirmations of the character you know you are but have yet to live out.**

Affirmations work because they condition the mind on where to place its focus. For most, living is generally regimented. From the moment you wake up to how you close the day, what happens in between is governed by set patterns or habits.

This is good up to a point. Habits are the brain's ultimate hack. Without this operating modality, you'd be frozen by the avalanche of stimuli that you come across every second.

However, habits become unhealthy and harmful when the former wiring is outdated. They no longer serve the individual's aspirations, desires, and needs.

To rewire the brain's existing system, repeat affirmations to yourself. The seeds of belief are thoughts. Affirmations are thoughts confidently spoken or asserted. Repetition transforms affirmations into new beliefs.

What you repeatedly think becomes who you are. Write who you believe you are and want to see in reality. Begin your statements with "I" plus an active verb.

Here are some example affirmations to incorporate speaking out as part of your identity.

- *I speak out for myself regardless of how others perceive me.*
- *I am my strongest advocate.*
- *I am unapologetically, authentically me.*

- *I say my truth in conversations and confrontations.*
- *I trust my voice and share my thoughts and feelings on my own terms.*

## Curiosity Takes Over Where Tenacity Ends.

There will come a point in your journey when sheer willpower, even when backed by a burning desire and a strong why, will flicker. It's not because you didn't do your best or somehow missed a vital step. It's because you gave your best. Your tank is running empty. You need to recharge. While recharging, there's an alternative fuel you can tap into to keep your momentum of progress. It can open doors tenacity can't. It's curiosity.

Curiosity is a strong desire to know or learn something. It's focused on what could be without needing to resolve what was or justifying what is. It allows you to be accepting of things outside of your control. It moves you into observation and wonder. You loosen the grip on controlling timelines. You enter into a state of flow. In this state, you abound with creativity. You see connections you haven't seen before. The storm may be treacherous, yet you are not threatened by it. You're enveloped by the fascination of the happening and unfolding scenes. You become attuned to what is and what could be next without forcing an outcome. You allow serendipities and miracles to reveal themselves to you.

Tenacity is like directing a horse to jump over fences. On the other hand, curiosity makes you get off the horse. It inspires you to watch what the horse would do when faced with an obstacle. It lets you accept who or what else would come to the horse's aid when a brick wall—seemingly insurmountable things outside your control—shows up along the journey.

Being curious takes you out of the film and makes you part of the captivated audience. With this third-party perspective, you see the bigger picture. You notice your blind spots, areas that others see but you weren't able to see when you were in character. You increase your self-awareness. Self-awareness is key to rediscover who you were before the world put a label on who you should be.

Get curious about your reactions and responses. Example statements and questions that evoke curiosity include the following:

- "I wonder what makes me stay silent when I have something to say."
- "I'm curious why I respond with no when asked if there was something wrong."
- "What makes me say, 'I'm fine' when I'm clearly not?"
- "I wonder why my heart thumps when I'm about to share my thoughts in public."
- "What makes me say yes even when the request crosses my boundaries?"

Curiosity opens you up to get to know your tendencies and the underlying narratives that inform these.

Curiosity also ignites imagination. Imagination is an underrated superpower in creating the path for a future that is vastly different from where you seem to be heading. Einstein captured this essential power best when he uttered, "Imagination is everything. It is the preview of life's coming attractions."

You can create a version of the future you desire when you stretch and act on your imaginations. Steve Jobs said it best: "Life can be much broader once you discover one simple fact: Everything around you that you call life was made up by people that were no smarter than you. And you can change it, you can influence it. Once you learn that, you'll never be the same again."

**Flex Your Curiosity Muscles by Previewing a Day in the Life of Your 90-Year-Old Self.**

Read the following instructions before doing the activity.

Sit comfortably with your shoulders down and back. Gently close your eyes if you're comfortable. Otherwise, you can lower your gaze toward the floor.

Imagine you are walking by the seashore. You can smell the salty air. You can feel the sand under your feet and in between your toes. It's warm and breezy today. There are not too many people by the beach. You get to enjoy the sound of the waves and seagulls flying nearby.

About an arm's length from you appears a teal door with brass knobs. You open the door and you see evergreen trees. You enter through the door, and as you look down, you notice a spiral staircase. You walk down.

Upon reaching the end of the stairwell, you see a golden door. You open it and see it's a private theatre room. You go in and sit on one of the plush loveseats. The feature that's playing is a day in the life of your 90-year-old self. It starts with her waking up in the morning.

What is your 90-year-old self thinking about first thing in the morning? What are the exciting things she will be experiencing today? Who are the people around her, and how does she feel about them? What memories does she revisit throughout the day that make her feel proud of the life she's lived? Does she have a pet she hangs out with regularly? What are her hobbies? What are the three things she's most grateful for today? What is the one thing she would advise her younger self to start, stop, and keep doing? If you're torn now between two paths, which one would make her regret the least?

The movie ends. You feel inspired. You have new ideas on what could lead to a life you'll love at ninety. You open the golden door and walk up the stairs, feeling pensive. You open the teal door and you're back by the seashore.

How would you live today knowing that your actions determine your future self's well-being and quality of life?

Queen, will you start to speak out for yourself?

### Compassion Picks Up Where Curiosity Ends.

When you're still recharging your tenacity tank with willpower and the inspiration from curiosity withers, let compassion be the fuel that keeps you on this growth journey. Being kind to yourself is a strategy to stay with the process. If you talk down to yourself for not being tenacious or curious enough, you'll prematurely end your practice.

The road to rediscover your voice will be longer than your buffered expectations. It'll have twists and turns that you can't foresee. If you keep rooting for yourself, though, you're more likely to keep taking one chance after another. When these chances accumulate, you'll wake up one day realizing that speaking out has become natural, easy, and a part of your lifestyle.

You'll make mistakes. You'll feel like you're not evolving fast enough. You'll see others who seem to get it done without delay. You'll feel small and inadequate. Be gentle with yourself.

Becoming your own advocate and champion is a personal journey. There are many factors that inform how soon and how much pain you go through before this becomes your way of life.

Learn from your toddler self. When she was learning to walk, did she curse at herself for falling down? No. She was okay with trying and falling. She gave herself unspoken grace. Look at where you are now because of her self-compassion. Unless you've lost your ability to walk, you're likely walking without thinking about it. Thank yourself for showing up for you. Gratitude is an antidote to giving up.

## The Trifecta Qualities of a Queen Who Speaks Out

You're now aware of a Queen's trifecta qualities for speaking out. Amidst the external and internal barriers you encounter, develop tenacity. Engage curiosity. Have compassion for yourself. You're on your way to becoming the champion of your authentic self.

# CHAPTER 2

## Your Self-Silencing Is Negatively Impacting Your Well-Being

**LIFE HASN'T BEEN EASY.** You've felt hurt and afraid. You've struggled to feel hope and doubted if you were going to get through this current state and overcome. You want to feel free, joyful, confident, and powerful. Yet the voices in your mind keep harping that you can't. You're not worthy.

Shame and guilt cloud your truth. They weigh heavy on you and you're tired. The fighting has drawn out. Pressing on feels daunting. You want to let the feelings go yet each time you do, they come back seemingly more intense than before.

Your feelings are valid.

I'm sorry you're feeling isolated. It's okay to feel how you feel. You need an ally who accepts your thoughts and feelings as they are. You can seek a guide who can help strengthen and empower you with what you need when you need to access them.

May these words travel far and reach you at the right time because I want them to remind you of truths about you. You're loved. You're worthy. You're enough. You're powerful. You matter. You're not too much. You're not insane. You have hope and love within you. You can do this. You will do this.

There's one skill to learn, relearn, and get better at—speaking out for yourself. You're going to need to stand up for what's within you if you want to live a life that's true to who you are.

This is likely not what you observed growing up. You've witnessed women in your life hide their real voices to save face in order to retain a respected position in their community. You've been trained to be quiet. You've been taught to accept others' perspectives as superior to yours. But this pattern must end with you because this self-silencing habit causes immense suffering and robs you of a great life.

Seek ways to rest and recover. You need your energy to create and protect a life you love. Speaking out for yourself is the engine you need to start driving your life. A more hopeful future requires you to steer toward an intended destination versus drifting along with others' opinions on how you ought to be and live.

Wearing a fake persona to keep others comfortable when you're crumbling inside can seem inconsequential. Yet, you can only deny your needs for so long.

Over time, they compound. As they do, tension within builds up into stress. Chronic stress hurts each aspect of your life—leading to degraded overall health and well-being, pain and strain in relationships, reduced productivity and creativity, and poor financial health.

## What You Think You're Protecting Is Compromised When You Silence Your Truth.

Keeping quiet was a tactic employed to maintain a false sense of peace and comfort. You didn't rock the boat even when water was flooding in. You slipped and bruised but still say you're okay. Self-sacrificing women were elevated. Inconvenient honesty was branded unnecessary.

Where did this *Keep Silent* culture get humanity? According to the World Health Organization in January 2020, "Depression is a leading cause of disability worldwide and is a major contributor to the overall global burden of disease. More women are affected by depression than men." Suppressing emotions and thoughts is associated with an increased risk for depression.

If speaking out for yourself forms a foundation to healthy living, why is it seldomly done? One of the reasons is that many believe a myth: "Speaking out will ruin peace, which could destroy what matters most—relationships, source of income, and good daily living."

### Relationships Are Nurtured When Each

### Individual's Truth Is Shared.

The quality of your closest relationships greatly impacts your quality of life. When your relationships are thriving, you feel safe, secure, and unstoppable. When they are deteriorating, you feel insecure, discouraged, and distracted. It's rightful for you to be protective of your relationships. Yet, it's not through self-silencing that you cultivate them.

Conflict is inevitable when unique individuals who are bound to have different views come together. There's often a choice to be made: to speak out your truth or succumb to silence when disagreements arise. When silence is chosen with small things, it becomes the go-to decision on bigger topics. What starts out as benign becomes malignant. From there, it spreads and is difficult to address and manage.

What starts out as resolvable conflicts become irreconcilable differences. The last recourse can be to sever ties or endure hellish existence should you choose to stay in what had become a toxic environment. Either choice causes grief and devastation to all parties involved.

Relationships, especially chosen ones like friendships, partnerships, marriage, employment, and community memberships, generally don't start out unbearable. However, actions compound and they become habits. Habits are automatic responses that require little to no thought.

At first, people get away with few inconveniences. Then, these inconveniences turn into boundary-crossing behaviors. If these continue, the habit problem evolves into a character flaw, which becomes intolerable. By this time, however, they're ingrained in the person and would require tremendous effort and time to reconstruct the pattern. It becomes monumental to influence them at this point.

How people perceive you is how they'll treat you. Absent your self-assertions, others won't have an alternative view to consider. You can speak out on what you stand for. You can make known what are acceptable and unacceptable ways to relate with you. You can set and enforce boundaries. What you can't do is control the filter through which they see. It'll still be up to them to evolve their thinking. They can still choose to have fixed mindsets. And how they choose to think and behave isn't your burden to carry.

To illustrate the impact of not speaking out in relationships, let's take a look at a few common issue topics and example scenarios in marriage and parent-adult child relationships.

### Not Speaking Out Ruins a Marriage.

Money is a point of contention for many couples. It's one of the top reasons for separations (Ramsey 2017). It starts with one party having loose spending habits while the other tends to save more than spend. One can make snide remarks about the buying behavior of their partner. The spender feels irritated and subdued. The saver perceives that their partner is acting selfishly and being inconsiderate.

Instead of talking about expectations and parallel emotions, you dismiss the remarks to not start an argument. A few more occurrences happen and you keep avoiding discussion. Two parties feel misunderstood and undervalued. Over time, negative feelings fester. When left unprocessed, this turns into resentment. Resentment weakens the intimate bond between partners.

You start nitpicking over unrelated things at home, play the blame game, become vindictive, or numb your feelings in unhealthy ways. Unspoken and unprocessed feelings and thoughts cause a widening rift in the relationship. The next thing you know, you wake up with a once-cherished relationship turning sour and becoming a nightmare.

This scenario also applies with differences in worldview, values, lifestyles, goals, and childrearing preferences.

**Not Speaking Out Destroys Your**

**Bond with Your Parents.**

Even as an adult, you may still find it hard to disagree with your parents' guidance. You know that they have your best interests in mind. Yet, you want to make decisions that are more driven by your preferences and vision of your future versus theirs. However, to appease and please your parents, you don't speak out your truth. You keep doing what they've pressured you to do.

Years down the road, you become unhappy, unsatisfied, and untrue to your own self. This path, while perceived as safe and stable, leads you to misery and discontentment. Regret festers. Blame begins. Resentment arises. You try to stay respectful toward your parents. Yet there's hatred brewing. You dislike yourself for the negativity you feel toward them. It's eating your joy, peace, and self-esteem.

As you chronically conceal your truth, you begin to self-doubt. The more you doubt yourself, the more you lose your sense of personal identity and agency. It may even dawn on you that you don't recognize yourself anymore. When this happens, there's a big chance you'll seek drastic measures to transform your life. You cut ties. You avoid visiting with them.

What you think you're protecting by silencing yourself can be what you give up to feel good and like your old self again.

## You Unintentionally Withhold the Gift of Growth by Not Speaking Out.

You may dread giving negative reviews of how others are doing. Yet, without constructive critiques, they likely won't grow, expand, and mature as much as they're capable of.

Speaking out has the refining power to hold a mirror to someone. It allows them to see themselves as they're perceived. It can be the push and motivation they need to seek help, progress, or change course for growth. They can always choose to consider your advice without the burden of following you.

One of the people I got into a lot of disagreements with was my younger sister, Lauriz Ann. She spoke her truth even when it was different to mine. Her words sometimes stung. I felt defensive and angry. They were also clarifying. It moved me to identify the inflexible and flexible topics I'm closed and open to discuss.

I got curious on what drove my initial reactions to my sister's words. With reflection, I learned the obsolete narratives I kept repeating to myself that needed upgrading. I grew from the temporarily hurtful discourse. My sister's voice was one of the growth catalysts in my journey.

When others stop caring, they stop correcting. The quote by Randy Pausch, in his book *The Last Lecture*, rings true: "When you're screwing up and nobody says anything to you anymore, that means they've given up on you…You may not want to hear it but your critics are often the ones telling you they still love you and care about you and want to make you better."

There are instances when you may reconsider speaking out your feedback. Pause when the other person is hurting. Stop when they continue to show they're not listening. After you shared your piece, you've released the gift. It's up to them to claim or disregard it.

## At Work, You Leave Peace and Promotion on the Table When You Don't Speak Out.

Half of your waking moments or more are spent working. Yet many are not completely satisfied with what they do for a living (Gallup 2020). Seven of ten women said sexual harassment is a major problem at work (Gallup 2019). Are you feeling disengaged or resigned from what you do? Does the work day feel like a drudgery? Do you feel unsafe at work? You're not alone.

There are many factors outside your control that lead to work disengagement. One element within your influence is speaking out for yourself. Yes, it is hard. And creativity and productivity thrive with open and honest communication. When you don't share your truth, the team misses out on your insights. Believe it. Your voice helps ignite and scale your organization's desired outcomes.

Every talent's truth collectively expressed and heard gives the company an irrefutable, competitive edge. Humanity embedded in how you serve and the products you sell becomes the secret sauce that acts as a lever. It positions you well to thrive. It makes you stand out, be seen, and be overwhelmingly preferred by your prospective clients, customers, and strategic partners.

In disagreements with your boss or coworkers, it may be tempting to be quiet. You go with their perspective without expressing what you think and feel. When you do this, your silence is sabotaging both of your successes.

When you keep quiet at the outset, it sets a tone for how you work. You're perceived as a yes-woman. People-pleasing feels comfortable because it's what you've always known. Yet, it isn't a leadership trait. It's a barrier that keeps you from thriving. It acts as a wedge between you and opportunities for expanded roles, challenging assignments, and an upward career mobility.

When evaluating for promotion to higher leadership positions, your visibility and assertiveness matter. When you keep quiet, your voice is muted. When it's muted, you're hidden. When you're hidden, your name doesn't come up during promotion deliberations.

People watch, observe, and make judgments about you with each encounter. How do you deal with challenging personalities or situations? Do you habitually act on your emotions? It's one thing to feel. Feelings are valid. It's another thing to give in to them. When feeling bad, do you default to lash out or cower? In trying situations, take a pause and breathe deeply. When you're calm and ready, firmly speak your truth.

Speaking out is a superpower that makes your latent capabilities obvious to you and others. It doesn't imply getting your way, while this can happen as a result. What ends up happening can look different from what you think it should be. This is common. What's paramount is that you share your thoughts and advocate for yourself.

## In Your Business or Side Hustle, You Lose Income and Impact When You Don't Speak Out.

Fostering a community around your message and movement is imperative to a solid business. How often do you show up to build rapport and nurture productive relationships with your target audience? Sharing behind-the-scenes information, funny or inspiring experiences, lessons you've learned along the way, and troubles you've gone through and solved draw your people closer to you. The closer people feel toward you, the more they'll support and buy into your brand or business.

You can choose any medium, as long as you remain authentic and share consistently. Start engaging at least once a week. Aim to tell your truth to your audience once a day once you've passed the inevitable learning curves with technology and systems.

Selling is another form of speaking out that's part of having a business. It's persuading a potential client to enroll in your paid solution. Closing deals and partnerships require it.

It's normal to feel intimidated to sell. To gain confidence, reframe what selling means. It's not being sleazy or greedy. It's a vital process for your business to exist and scale its impact. It's a must-do for your message and movement to have staying power.

When you know you're providing 10x the value of what you're charging, it's a disservice not to sell. Your customer needs what you have to provide. It's the solution they've been seeking to go from where they are to where they want to be. Your job is to inspire, educate, motivate, and call them to begin or stay in the journey to their desired end state. Sell in order to make things happen for you and them.

Pitching your offering once won't move the needle in getting to your profit and revenue goals. Making it part of your daily to-do list will. Seek systems and processes that embed selling into your operations. Hire a dedicated sales team when scaling.

### Your Self-Silencing Makes Your Relationships Prone to Breaking.

There are two types of stress you encounter in relationships in life and at work—internal system stress and external stress. Internal system stress includes disagreements within the team, mismatched expectations, lack of empathy, and blurry vision. External stress looks like the COVID-19 pandemic, extreme market fluctuations, and natural disasters.

External stressors are far out of your range to change. They tend to be disastrous at once yet occur infrequently. Internal system stressors, on the other hand, are like paper cuts. They are tiny jabs that don't knock you out at once. Instead, they repeatedly sting, exhaust, distract, and throw you off course.

To withstand external stress, build your internal system's resilience. Resilience is the ability to bounce back after falling. It's a prerequisite to a life lived well despite constant struggles. To build internal resilience, timely address internal system stress. Use your voice. Leverage your words. Communicate your truth. Hold a safe space to debate and deliberate opposing views. Queen, speak out! As the famous quote says, "Nip it in the bud." Take care of the small things so they don't fester and become larger issues.

Fragility is the opposite of resilience. It's the quality of being easily broken or damaged. Relationships become fragile when there are more unknowns than knowns. More truth between parties are hidden than are revealed. There's no safe space to release, contradict, argue fairly, and love while disagreeing amongst each other. Nicks and scrapes, hurtful exchanges, and misunderstandings are left unattended and exposed to dirt and further tears.

When you keep your voice locked within, you're setting up your physical and mental health, relationships, and work to shatter in the face of unpredictable external stressors that are bound to occur. Challenges are ever present, and a fragile system is prone to crumbling and dissolution.

Provide immediate and specific feedback following an event to members of your team, your boss, your partner, and coworkers. Take out the emotion and stay as objective as you can. Remind yourself that not speaking out will cause more critical issues later on than being upfront now.

## You Have the Power to Positively Influence Women Toward Boldness and Self-Advocacy.

What starts with you changes the world, whether you see the reach of your impact or not. The ripple effect of your growth in character and self-healing will likely remain elusive to you. Yet it doesn't mean you're not making a difference in this world and the generations to come. Every human is within six degrees of separation from each other. We are intertwined in a complex ecosystem. What you do or don't do affects the trajectory of humanity's health and total well-being.

Values are mainly learned through observation versus narratives. When you speak out for yourself, you set a different standard. You establish a new benchmark for how you and others ought to be treated—one that elevates respect for women now and into the future. You build on the work done by female warriors before you. As Margaret Mead, American cultural anthropologist, eloquently stated, "Never doubt that a small group of thoughtful, committed citizens can change the world. Indeed, it is the only thing that ever has."

People are observing even when you don't notice that they are. Your voice matters and it needs to be released. You may be wrong or right. Regardless, your feelings remain valid and need to be shared. Open yourself up to being heard, having a seat at the tables of your choice, and leaning in.

Speaking out goes against the current of cultural and societal norms, as we'll see in the next chapter. Yet change is possible and necessary. We're at the inflection point in history. We're living in the #metoo era. Let's keep pushing forward to honor the sacrifices and hard work that our female ancestors did to get us here. Let's set up ourselves and future Queens for a life unbounded by their gender.

# CHAPTER 3
# How Did You End Up Not Speaking Out for Yourself

IT'S NOT YOUR FAULT that you default to sidestepping your own truth and voice. Most women have been conditioned to keep their thoughts and feelings to themselves. For some, it's because well-meaning people in their lives wanted to make them feel safe and accepted by society and culture. For others, it's because ill-intentioned people stole women's voices due to unchecked ignorance, an oversized ego, envy, lust, greed, and hunger for power. They silenced women to keep them oppressed. Either way, you ended up not speaking out for yourself because of external pressures that you internalized as your own set of beliefs.

## Reason #1. Well-Meaning People Trained You Not to Speak Out for Yourself.

The majority of societies in the world adopted a patriarchal system in which men were viewed as superior to women. While the more overt expression of this system has been dismantled in many regions, deep-seated beliefs and practices remain pervasive.

For most of human history, women have been conditioned to put a premium on others' opinions over their own. It's a worldview ingrained into the psyche and handed down from one generation to another.

You were taught to care about what other people thought of you more than what you thought of yourself. You were forced to deny your voice the opportunity to get airtime while others' ideas comfortably took up space. You were influenced to doubt your thinking and feelings. You were repeatedly prompted to consult with others for their validation, approval, and permission prior to saying or doing anything.

For some, your well-meaning parents or guardians, teachers, and elders were the ones who taught you not to speak out for yourself. This mindset was reinforced in the entertainment you consumed as a child up until your adulthood. In communities, you observed this way of life espoused by women you loved and admired.

Speaking out for yourself was an unattractive irregularity in your circle. Those who spoke out tended to be the social pariahs. They were labeled as disrespectful and selfish—looking out only for themselves at the expense of others' well-being. They were also branded as unduly emotional and sensitive, unable to take hold of their own selves.

If their speaking-out style was meek, their input wasn't considered seriously. Wearing their hearts on their sleeves was seen as a liability. If they were assertive, they were painted as witches, scolded or rejected in social circles. Neither outcomes of speaking one's truth seemed worth deviating from the norm. So instead, most kept silent on their thoughts and feelings. They went with the flow instead of creating a necessary ruckus.

When your basic human need for love, belonging, physical safety, and security were on the line, you didn't risk going against the grain. Patriarchy and toxic masculinity prevailed despite them being harmful to the community.

Humiliation trained women to devalue themselves. It resulted in degraded self-belief. Learned helplessness became a mental prison that was unconsciously impossible to escape. Your ancestral mother was manipulated into this lifestyle. So was your grandmother, mother, and now you. It was a strategic move by men in power to preserve hierarchy, top-of-the-pyramid positions, authority, and control over society, institutions, organizations, homes, and ways of living.

Ideas that challenged authority were a threat to the

controlling power. To contain this threat, those who spoke out with contrarian thoughts were punished with rejection and isolation. Those who kept mum and tolerated patriarchy got rewarded. Incentives such as food, clothes, shelter, love, belonging, social status, employment, promotion, or recognition were doled out as coveted prizes for not speaking out. Basic human needs were withheld from those who vocalized their truth. It was a perpetuated psychological manipulation that has been disintegrating over time yet still has roots spread wide.

Those who loved and wanted the best for you saw that if you broke away from tradition, you may be deemed an outcast. You may get criticized. You may lose opportunities for financial rewards and social status. So, they encouraged you to stay in bounds. "Keep your head down. Stay silent. Suck it up," they advised. You're not one to let strangers intimidate you into subversion. However, when those closest to you advised you not to speak out for yourself, it felt unbearable, yet you were unable to resist it. You hid your voice.

Your closest loved ones may have had a savior's complex. They longed to be needed and useful. Instead of teaching you to fight for yourself, they found their purpose and identity in looking after you. Even when you didn't ask them to solve a problem, they went ahead and did it anyway. It's a mindset also called the "white knight syndrome."

Marilyn Krueger and Mary Lumia defined white knight syndrome, in their book by the same name, "as a destructive need to rescue others usually from themselves." You may have been raised by a parent with this trait. You didn't get the opportunity to develop your own voice because someone else spoke out for you more often than not. You may have had a significant other who spoke out for you, thinking that they were saving you. Unknowingly, this behavior diminished your self-confidence and ability to rescue your own self. You got accustomed to someone else representing you so you became intimidated to choose and advocate for yourself.

## Reason #2. Narcissists Robbed You of Your Voice.

Devastatingly, many have suffered at the hands of a narcissist: someone who thinks the world revolves around them. You can spot a narcissist by their excessive need for admiration, disregard for others' feelings, an inability to tolerate any criticism, and a sense of entitlement. Their unresolved conflicts within themselves lead them to heap abuse on others.

Your voice serves as a carrier for your potential to be realized. Without this carrier, your gifts remain hidden and unused. Your potent gifts are a threat to narcissists, who like to maintain the abusive environment that serves their diseased egos. To prevent you from awakening to your gifts, they confused, humiliated, and made you doubt your truth. As part of your journey to reclaim your voice, it's prudent to get to know the thieves and their stealing tactics. Paraphrasing the great military strategist Sun Tzu, you'll best defeat the enemy you know well.

Here are some of the patterns, behaviors, and traits of the abusers who steal women's voices.

- **They're miserable and they want company in their misery.** There could be many reasons for their misery. They may have had unprocessed trauma. They could have failed at attempts to make something meaningful out of their lives. Instead of getting back up, pivoting, and progressing, they wallowed in their defeat and embraced the victim mentality. They were unable to unveil their gifts, so now they want you to hide yours too. If you spoke out your truth, you may find out there's a different, more fruitful way to live. Then, you'd pack up and leave, and the thief will end up alone in their misery. This is why they keep anchoring you.

- **They're projecting their fears on you.** To the thief, your voice screams danger. Your speaking out your truth is a threat to their current standing, which is built on sand. There's no wonder why they aggressively mobilize their network and resources to keep you from talking. For when you talk and keep sharing your truth, the walls of their kingdoms shake. They become vulnerable to face the consequences of their wrongdoings, weaknesses, and limitations. To see that they're ordinary humans— and not gods as they made themselves believe—is their greatest fear. They'd much prefer to carry their false armor than to face their true self in the mirror. Therefore, they manipulate you into being silent.

- **They can only keep their control over you so long as you believe your value lies with them versus your inner self.** The moment you value speaking out for yourself over pleasing others, they lose their noose on your life. You will, in turn, inspire others to talk, and that makes them sweat bullets. There's power in a multitude who speaks out for themselves, and the narcissist knows it. They will pit women against women as a divisive strategy to prevent a pack of lionesses from coming together and annihilating their perceived superiority. These abusers defined and established artificial standards for attractiveness. They promoted comparisons to keep the focus on where you are in the ladder versus whether the ladder is even worth climbing or not. They created systems to keep themselves and people like them in power. It's cleverly crafted and conniving.

- **They have a fixed mindset and believe in a zero-sum game.** If you win, they believe they'll lose. The only way they keep winning is if you keep losing. They're unable to see how the world can hold a multitude of spaces for many groups of people to win and not only a few. When you open up your thoughts and feelings, you enter the arena to fight for yourself instead of lingering as a bystander in your own life. When you play, there's a chance you may win. They see this as a threat to their dominion and can't tolerate that risk; therefore, they make it unappealing for you to speak out.

Voice repression is used to perpetuate oppression. Gaslighting is a psychological and emotional manipulation technique narcissists employ to keep you self-silencing. What are the gaslighting signs, symptoms, and strategies?

- **Discrediting.** They'll discredit your character to invalidate your voice. They do this by smearing your reputation and accusing you of having selfish motives for speaking out, such as seeking attention, fame, or payout. Notice that when men sue others, it's labeled as "fighting for justice." When women do it, we're branded as "yearning for attention."

- **Victim blaming and shaming.** When survivors come out to testify against their abusers, they're blamed and shamed. Instead of being empowered and encouraged, they get blamed for the perpetrators' evil deeds. "It was your fault" is an all too common hurtful and damaging excuse. "You were at the wrong place, wearing the wrong clothes, speaking the wrong words" are the statements thrown on the open wounds of survivors. The abused are often not believed. Others assume their version of the truth is more believable than that of the victim.

- **Casting Doubt.** Narcissists will make you believe that nobody will believe what you'll say. They'll deceive you into believing that speaking out won't matter because there isn't enough evidence to prove you're right. They know you're speaking the truth, but to suppress your voice, they want you to doubt yourself. So they question you: "How can you be sure? Are you certain you're not making these things up in your mind?" Casting doubt is a tactic to fragment your inner power. When you doubt yourself, you divide your energy, focus, and strength. Once you become fragmented, you're weakened. It's how the perpetrators defeat you. They use your mind against itself.

- **Labeling.** When you stand up and speak out for yourself for being unfairly treated, they'll tell you that you're crazy, acting irrational, being emotional, or worse, call you a b*tch. There's currently no level of accomplishment that makes a woman immune from getting branded negatively when they voice their dissents.

- **Deflecting.** When you're strongly advocating for yourself, a narcissist will tell you to calm down or relax. They'll say that their insulting words were a joke and that you're too sensitive to take one. Your self-consciousness gets triggered. Then they'll change topics in hopes you'll forget what you were advocating. These manipulations are a form of deflection to downplay their assaulting comments. They also act as an alibi so the narcissist can avoid confronting their misdoings. They put the burden on you to push your feelings aside instead of them directly apologizing and committing not to say offensive comments in the future.

- **Distraction.** While you're making a point, they may distract you with their nonverbal gestures, showing disrespect or contempt. They could be fidgeting, playing with their phones, looking at their watches, or eye-rolling. Some do this without being intentionally hurtful, yet intention doesn't equate impact. These gestures are demoralizing and keep your focus away from fully expressing your thoughts and emotions, making you feel unworthy of attention and invisible. They could also say comments that throw you off focus. Some common ones that cause you to be even more agitated include, "You seem angry." or "You're making this a big deal."

- **Mansplaining.** Due to a false presumption that men's voices are more credible than yours, they explain to you condescendingly or in a patronizing manner a topic that you know more about. They interrupt or speak over you. This happens often on topics ranging from men explaining feminism to women, having your field of expertise explained to you, or someone who doesn't know you, insisting you'll love a particular thing. This behavior can cause you to doubt the value of your own voice and whether you should speak out for yourself or not.

- **Lying and Denial.** When you confront a narcissist with a mistreatment or abuse and all their other tactics fail, they'll flat out lie, withhold a significant portion of the truth, or deny they've committed acts of wrongdoing. Because many assaults and mistreatment on women occur when either no one else is around but the perpetrator and the survivor or when they are with complicit individuals, survivors get discouraged to speak out for themselves.

As you've seen above, the expert mental maneuvers make it extremely difficult to speak out for yourself consistently. However, awareness of these makes you more likely to spot them when they occur and apply countermoves that we'll discuss in later chapters.

With words, narcissists steal freedoms. With words, they rob women of their path to create a life they love and change the world. With words, you'll take back your power and destiny for yourself, fellow Queens, and the generations that come after you.

### Reason #3. You Believe in Myths About Speaking Out for Yourself.

Oppressors are the purveyors of women's self-silencing. However, your unconscious beliefs in myths about speaking out also contribute in pulling you back from having a voice. These beliefs are conclusions derived from mainstream examples of what speaking out for yourself should look like.

- **Myth #1. You have to be extroverted or loud to have a voice.** The examples you've seen in media and communities show that speaking out is reserved for those with a loud voice or an extroverted personality. Their booming voice reverberates from one end of the room to the other. They may not need a microphone to project what they say. When you're quiet, reserved, or introverted, you may believe you don't have a voice. This is a myth. You can be quiet, have a soft voice, and speak out for yourself.

In her TEDx Talk, "Quiet People Will Change the World," Sara Dahan, veteran community builder, founder, and CEO of Catalyst, explained it well when she said, "People assumed that because I was quiet that I didn't have a voice or a stake in the conversation, but quiet people have immense power… Quietness is my superpower. I didn't build these communities despite being a quiet introvert. I built them because I am a quiet introvert. I leaned into who I am. I listened, observed, and reflected to become a more kind and effective connector…If you are a quiet person, you can start by putting yourself out there…Gain confidence in what you want to say by practicing the art of conversation."

- **Myth #2. You have to speak out in public.** You see people who speak out in public and assume that to speak out for yourself means to do it in a group or with a big audience. So when you speak out in private, you assume these don't count. However, the number of people in your audience is not a basis for speaking out. You may speak out your truth through journaling, emailing, direct messaging, texting, and handwriting notes as well as meeting with others one-on-one.

- **Myth #3. You have to speak out on all issues.** Because people who speak out seem to be the ones who have a perspective or opinion on a variety of topics, you assume that to speak out for yourself, you, too, have to be opinionated on every issue under the sun. You don't have to speak out on everything. You can choose as few or as many topics as you want to share your thoughts or feelings. The number of topics you give your perspective to is not a basis for speaking out.

- **Myth #4. You have to speak out now.** While it's important to speak out for yourself in a timely manner, it doesn't have to be done immediately if you don't feel safe at the moment of the event. Yes, there's a chance that you may get used to delaying. Yes, the impact of your perspective may be reduced the longer from the incident you wait before you speak out. However, there are matters that take time for you to even begin to process, especially with traumatic experiences.

  You determine when it's a good time for you to speak out. Let no one pressure you into speaking out in the same way they've pressured you to be silent. You own your behavior and responses. You decide and choose what best fits your needs and intentions for any given moment.

- **Myth #5. You have to be perfect.** Because speaking out comes with a potential for backlash, you assume that you have to wait to have it all together before you can speak out. This is far from the truth. It's unrealistic to aim for perfection. Perfection is the ultimate excuse not to speak out. There's no preparation that can get you to perfection. Imperfect people speak out to begin healing, not after being fully healed. They speak out to express their inner power, not after becoming a powerful person.

It's not your fault that you've held your truth in for this long. Speaking out means rowing against the headwinds of culture, oppressors, and false narratives. Yet by recognizing the root of how you haven't let your voice out for what feels like an entire lifetime, you can begin to rediscover and reclaim it. Yes, at the beginning of this journey you'll experience fear. Yes, change doesn't happen overnight. And you have it in you to keep on keeping on. Because you're worthy of a life that honors your truth.

# PART TWO:

## Transform from Within

# CHAPTER 4

## You Can Choose to Free Your Voice

**FREEING YOUR VOICE** looks like leaving a metaphorical cage. Some are temporary while others are permanent. A temporary leave is taking an extended break from your routines to reimagine your situation. You can take a solo vacation, staycation, or weekend getaway. Away from the usual, you deliberately get curious about how your life is going. You explore creative ways to keep an existing relationship, home address, or work commitment while becoming free to be you. You journal your thoughts and feelings without judgment or guardrails. Your goal is clarity in thinking, direction, and next steps.

Permanent departures include quitting a job, moving to a new home, or ending a relationship. You lose something old and familiar to give space to new ways of living. Because of the magnitude of consequences, give yourself ample time to process thoughts and emotions. In between having the idea and making moves, consistently check with your intuition. When you gain the same answer after several check-ins, follow your gut.

A day before Juneteenth 2020, I felt a tight knot tying my guts. Bitter juice was climbing up my throat. No amount of water would bring it back down. My heart was racing. I was lying on my back on a hand-woven rug in the middle of my one-bedroom apartment's living room. I had to make the decision that I've been seriously exploring for a couple of years. I sensed the need to quit a job in a career path where I invested tremendous personal capital to build—years living away from my husband.

The timing seemed inappropriate. We were still early in the COVID-19 pandemic without foresight on how long it would last. I had organizations and a business to support during this turbulent time. My husband's company was also struggling. I didn't have adequate cash reserves that would make me feel financially secure. My ideas for what could be my next step were not yet in full motion. I didn't have another income stream to replace what I was earning as an employee. Leaving a comfortable, six-figure job should've been the last thing on my mind.

It wasn't like I hated my job or the company. I created and advocated to have this role. I was supported by my leaders. I was learning tremendously. And if I wanted, I could find a new role within the company relatively quickly as I had earned my place as a top talent in the organization. There was potential for an upward mobility. I didn't think I was completely stuck. Yet, the pull to do my calling and pursue it at this season was stronger than the long list of cons wrapping around my one pro.

What I couldn't explain was a knowing in me that things will be okay. I trusted the Voice calling me, and I believed in my own voice. I shared with my trusted sponsors, mentors, manager, and peers my decision to leave. It was accepted with mixed emotions, but overall, I was understood.

When I disclosed my decision to my husband, Mike, it was painful at the outset. The resistance was strong. Mike is normally supportive with my personal choices, but due to financial instability, he didn't believe in the timing of this latest adventure. Even when quitting my job meant putting an end to our eight-year long-distance situation, he didn't immediately get behind it. He said hurtful things. While the words stung, I believed they were temporary. There was certainty within me that he'd turn around. He'd support this endeavor as he'd done with my previous ones. And if he didn't for a while, I had a deep sense that things were going to be okay.

To many who have known me over the past two decades, they assume that I was born speaking out my mind and standing up for myself. While I may have tenacious genes in me (thanks, Mom!), they were activated by deliberate practice over time.

I remember my first high-stake conversation that led me to learn the immense power of voice. I was ten years old, laying on a stiff sofa in the living room of my childhood home. Lights were out. With my eyes squeezed shut and tears occasionally flowing out, I fervently prayed to Jesus for hours past midnight for Dad to come home safely.

At three in the morning, I breathed a sigh of relief when the front door squeaked open. I knew it was my dad. He was finally home. I tried to hold back the words I'd been meaning to confess to him. With tears, I calmly asked, "Dad, where have you been? Why are you home late again?" With his breath reeking of alcohol, he firmly replied, "I don't need to answer you. You're not my mother. You're not my wife. You're only my child." Out burst the words I'd been hiding in me since Mom died of breast cancer a few months before this incident. To my horror, I forcefully replied, "Exactly, Dad. I'm only a child. Yet I'm the one taking care of our home and my siblings—your children. I know you're grieving. But you still have four children who love and need you." The good girl in me was terrified. I'm not one to talk back to any elder, let alone my father.

I don't have substantial recollection on what happened after I spoke those words. I remembered uncontrollably sobbing. The next day, Dad prepared breakfast for us. Since then, Dad has been our present, loving, and enduring support. The bond we had with him got even stronger. I won't know what life and my relationship with my dad would've looked like had I not spoken out for myself and my siblings that evening twenty years ago. This moment cemented in my mind that one person's truth is a force to be reckoned with in effecting change in her life.

You have this force within you. Your voice is a superpower. Only you can give this power wings to take you places you want to go. You can make the choice to free your voice. I'm here as a guide, and this book is one of the many tools you can use along the journey.

The journey will be hard. It will take time. It will be nonlinear. And you're worthy of choosing this path of freedom. In the process, you'll get to know yourself more intimately. You'll come face-to-face with your strengths and areas of opportunities. Toward the close of this season, your voice will take your other gifts (yes, you have more than one) to the world. Life won't be the same again. You'll feel empowered.

## Fear Will Need to Ride with You as You Brave the Future.

You got your guide. You'll collect tools along the way. You find and invite your girlfriends to keep you hyped up. Then you charge forward, right? Yes, and there's one more passenger that will come with you on the journey. It's unlikely you'd want it with you, but it'll join you in your brave journey anyway. Its name is fear.

There's a myth going around saying that to do something brave, you must first be fearless. If you wait until you overcome fear, you likely will be held in a forever loop of "Ready. Aim. Ready. Aim." You won't get to fire and go.

The solution? Let fear ride with you in your journey to rediscover your voice. It takes a backseat but it rides with you. Susan Jeffers sums it well when she wrote in her book of the same title, "Feel fear and do it anyway."

Fear is expected in life. It's a built-in protective mechanism in our body to maintain homeostasis, aka stability. Without homeostasis, the mind and body can't survive long term. Change or threat sets off the fear alarm. When you attempt to do things you're not used to doing, your body sends emergency nerve signals to your brain to stop you.

Fear, while part of our defense mechanisms, can also go haywire and overprotect us to the point of needless suffering. Instead of staying in the backseat, it can grab the steering wheel. It can erratically press the gas pedal and brakes as in the case in the fear of speaking out.

If you don't want to feel fear, don't attempt change. However, this is unrealistic and detrimental to your healing and growth. In life, one of the few things that's constant is change. Therefore, fear is inevitable.

## You'll Have to Leave Your Old Mindset of Keeping Silent.

Ideally, when you change, authorities in your life approve it. The world around you fervently supports your transformation. If you had a magic wand, change would be smooth. Your loved ones would cheer you on, hugging you as you bade farewell to your self-silencing habit. Your coworkers would lift you up and encourage you. Your clients would double down on your business. But alas, speaking out for yourself entails offering alternative viewpoints. Some may be perceived poorly by others, especially when they've become accustomed to you nodding yes on most things they ask of you.

I hesitated calling you to action. To leave your old way of keeping silent in favor of going on a journey to rediscover your voice comes with real costs. I've gone through many iterations of the repercussions—and it hurt. Some will exclude you. Others will abandon you. You'll be uninvited to things. Disapproval and seeing others' disappointment in your pursuit of growth will sting. You'll be misunderstood. You may be accused of being selfish. In other words, this path will be tough. There's no sugarcoating it.

You'll have to leave your proverbial cage without permission. The good girl you've been will get rattled by this endeavor. Seeking permission first had once been your lifeblood when doing things. You mostly did only what was approved. Instead, you'll have to embrace an inner rebel. You'll have to ask for forgiveness later if you end up being wrong.

You'll not deliver your voice with eloquence, fairness, and poise when you're starting out. A polished kind of delivery will take practice over time. Even when you eventually do say things clearly, concisely, and with graceful composure, others can still feel offended and reject your voice.

Speaking out for yourself is a big deal. You're right not to take it lightly. The moment you make a choice to speak out for yourself, the dissociation from your former ways will be painful. You'll renounce your old habit of staying silent. It will involve getting a backlash from people who love you and are threatened by you changing on them. You'll lose some access and privileges. You'll make others feel uncomfortable. Feeling alienated is a price for sharing your truth.

## Well-Meaning People Don't Always Know What's Best for You.

Diana Prince, whom Gal Gadot played in Wonder Woman, left the safety, peace, and beauty of Themyscira against her loving mother's wishes to go after her calling. With this action, she spoke out for herself. Ordinary people would be wise to follow Diana's lead to create a life that's true to who they are.

Well-meaning people may not always know what's best for you. Dig deep within; you know what's best for you. It's time to listen to your intuition and the still, small voice that you'll perceive in your mind during your quiet moments. It's appropriate to validate with your trusted data sources. Validation isn't the same as self-doubt.

You may have grown up with a good-girl image, and that might have served you well. Being labeled as the good one allowed you to be accepted, embraced, and even put on a pedestal by your community. Yet this persona became an anchor that hindered your character development. What once was a beautiful thing is now a stopgap to your evolution. With life, you don't stay the same. You evolve or deteriorate. If you stay too long in your comfort zone, you'll wither.

The good-girl image is dependent on others' definition of what constitutes being a good girl. This perspective is based on interpretations informed by the patterns they've been exposed to in life. It's largely developed within the context of what the generation went through and how they processed the events experienced. What worked for thirtysomething decades pre-COVID may not apply to the same age group living in what *Choose Yourself* author James Altucher dubbed as The Great Reset and the new normal created as you read this book.

If being a good girl means obedience without critical thinking, following without discussion or debate, and abiding by rules without question, you're set up for a quality of life less than what you're capable of and deserving to experience. The world, as you observe, is in an upheaval. To speak your truth is mandatory. How else will you contribute to changes in the world that would become foundational to your life for the remainder of this century?

A limited description and oversimplification of what you could talk about and who you could be are reserved for machines. A robot can live this way sustainably, but this is horrifically suffocating for a human being who must rapidly adapt to survive and thrive. Your points of view matter. Your voice needs to be heard and considered.

As you follow your own voice, you'll have blunders. You'll be a round peg who won't fit a square hole. You, then, must embrace temporary defeats as invaluable sources of insight for your becoming. The process will not be straightforward. That's by design. Your resiliency gets exercised and strengthened as uncertainties come your way. Owning up to your mistakes made because you dared greatly is confidence-building. When you know you can fail and you still choose to enter the arena of your life, you embody a warrior's mindset. This brings to mind one of my all-time favorite inspiring quotes by Teddy Roosevelt, famously known as "The Man in the Arena."

> "It is not the critic who counts; not the man who points out how the strong man stumbles, or where the doer of deeds could have done them better. The credit belongs to the man who is actually in the arena, whose face is marred by dust and sweat and blood; who strives valiantly; who errs, who comes short again and again, because there is no effort without error and shortcoming; but who does actually strive to do the deeds; who knows great enthusiasms, the great devotions; who spends himself in a worthy cause; who at the best knows in the end the triumph of high achievement, and who at the worst, if he fails, at least fails while daring greatly, so that his place shall never be with those cold and timid souls who neither know victory nor defeat."

## Anticipate Different Scenarios along

## Your Brave Journey.

There are two types of change. One is voluntarily initiated. The other type is what you didn't see coming. Either type disrupts your normal patterns and gives you the opportunity to shift gears. The likely outcomes when you venture out in open waters, such as when you rediscover your voice, include sinking, floating, swimming, or all of the above.

**1. To sink is to succumb to a difficult situation and lose confidence in your ability to overcome.**

When difficulties pile up or arise at the same time, sinking is highly probable. Paradoxically, the journey of speaking out can make you confront unfamiliar emotions and thoughts that you'll be tempted to bottle up. As you bottle up your emotions over time, your density increases. You become denser than before, and gravity pulls you downward.

A way to overcome sinking is to continuously let out what you're keeping within you. This is in spite of you swallowing some water in the process. At first, your progress seems negligible. Yet, as you persist, you become lighter with each self-revelation. Even without kicking and flapping, you can bubble up toward the surface. Then you catch breath again.

How may this look like when encountering a difficult situation in real life?

It could look like journaling your thoughts and feelings. Writing your thoughts out is a form of speaking out even when your audience is unseen. It could also look like recording voice notes for yourself or praying.

As you get comfortable with intimate self-disclosure, you can begin to speak out in private. You can seek a coach or therapist's professional support or confess your feelings and thoughts to a trusted confidante.

In time, you can introduce your alternative views with a broader audience. It may be during a one-on-one at work or with your close relationships. Then you can speak out more in group meetings.

Speaking out can be written, verbal, or in action.

## 2. To float is to get by and tolerate a difficult situation.

Speaking out what was formerly bottled in you can take you from sinking to floating. While staying afloat is better than sinking, it isn't desirable long term. Floating doesn't become an issue until it's chronic. You get by, yet you go nowhere. You're surviving but not thriving. It may not be apparent, but floating is exhausting physically, emotionally, mentally, and spiritually. You can get burned out, not because you went on overdrive, but because you underutilized your capabilities.

I was floating for about a year when my supposed dream job turned into a deterrent in the pursuit of my personal mission—to help heal humanity by 2099. Following advocating for myself to gain more experience and contributing in building new business models for a company I worked for, I attained my desired role. However, it wasn't too long until a major organizational shift persisted. For twelve months I kept speaking out in many ways, styles, and with people of different roles and varying levels. I shared proposals and pilot test results, pursued co-funding opportunities, and cross-sector partnerships. While I knew I wasn't sinking, I also wasn't moving forward in my mission. I was floating. In this case, I was able to bear the burden of stagnation for a year but not longer.

To sail forward, you'll have to switch out of floating mode. With new game plans, moves, and skills, you can swim.

## 3. To swim is to move forward despite the difficult situation.

Swimming, unlike floating, is proactive. You're not merely unloading what was previously kept within, you're now also actively moving toward a desired future by speaking out for your needs and wants despite the many headwinds you face.

It could look like what Monica Lewinsky shared in her TEDx Talk. She reclaimed her voice after being publicly shamed to silence for a decade. Here's an excerpt from her talk's transcript.

> "Why? Why now? Why was I sticking my head above the parapet?.... Because it's time. Time to stop tiptoeing around my past, time to stop living a life of opprobrium and time to take back my narrative.
>
> It's also not just about saving myself. Anyone who is suffering from shame and public humiliation needs to know one thing: You can survive it. I know it's hard. It may not be painless, quick or easy, but you can insist on a different ending to your story. Have compassion for yourself. We all deserve compassion and to live both online and off in a more compassionate world."

Queen Monica is now an anti-bullying activist who delivers speeches on the harmful effects of bullying. She also contributes to Bystander Revolution, an anti-bullying resource founded by another Queen, MacKenzie Scott.

At work, it could look like getting a 50 percent increase, first-class travel benefits, luxury accommodation in a five-star hotel, and a generous expense account from the same employer who let you go. It's what swimming looked like for Queen Karen Arrington as she shared in her book, *Your Next Level Life*.

Karen had lost her so-called dream job and was in the midst of an unemployment panic-state. Instead of sinking or staying afloat, she wrote up a proposal with the stipulations mentioned above. Her proposal was approved by the company CEO within six hours of sending the email.

Swimming could look differently for you in your current season and path. Queens Monica's and Karen's stories are a few of the many positive outcomes within your reach when you do speak out for yourself. Consider that there are upsides to speaking out that are beyond what you think is possible now.

The crux in your speaking-out journey is letting what's true for you come out of you. This is key for your growth and well-being. They need not align with the absolute or socially accepted truths.

You can rediscover your voice and be your biggest champion in life and at work. You will. You must. And when you arrive at the final chapter, my hope is for you to confidently and naturally say, "I am a Queen. I speak out for myself. That's what I do. That's who I am." Keep swimming, sister.

# CHAPTER 5
# Speaking Out and Self-Care

**THE HABIT OF SPEAKING OUT** for yourself involves keenly listening to and trusting what your body is signaling through feelings. When you're attuned to how you feel and you speak out on your needs, you help your body manage wisely the regular onslaught of distress.

From the moment you wake up until you go to sleep, you encounter varying levels of distress. Your body's tendency is to absorb and react to stress without filter or questions. It sends out signals so your brain can command the rest of the body to address the cause. It's how you pull back when you touch a hot surface, press brakes when a car before you stops suddenly, or take a nap when you feel exhausted.

When your brain overrides the body's signals for course correction without checking them, the body can get overloaded. When your systems are overloaded, it breaks down over time. Your body breaking down shows up as symptoms of sickness ranging from mild to severe, physical and mental.

The approach to live healthily in a world with seemingly unending streams of information and obstacles is different for each person and the season they face. Your seasons ebb and flow morning to afternoon to evening, day by day, month by month. There are seasons within a season as there are weather fluctuations in summer, spring, fall, or winter.

There'll be times when what's right for you is to optimize self-healing over growth. You seek solitude to reflect and process. You spend more time listening and being in nature than creating and building. You focus on activities that promote the body's natural healing abilities. Then there'll be seasons when you accelerate your growth and development, so you spend more of your time engaging and connecting with people. You double-down on building and iterating on your creations. You design systems and enlist teams to market, sell, and scale your offering and value.

How you approach life in seasons is up to you. Listen to your body. Speak out on behalf of yourself. What is best to do one moment may be the opposite in another. Give yourself permission to adapt and grow as the days and months unfold versus holding on to fixed expectations.

There are two meanings of speaking out that are covered in this chapter. One is to speak out to process your inner thoughts and feelings. Another is to speak out for yourself with others.

## Speaking Out Is Self-Care and It Is Not Selfish.

There's a place in your wellness practices for speaking out for yourself. For women, we've erred mostly on the side of self-suppression. To bring back real harmony and balance within you and in your life and work, you'll need to share your truth more often than not.

During a transition, you're ebbing and flowing in your mental and emotional states and energy levels at more heightened scales than before. Vocalize these peaks and valleys and refuse to suppress them. When you're feeling tired, hurt, lost, anxious, afraid, confused, annoyed, or frustrated, let it out in your preferred manner. When you're feeling happy, grateful, content, loving, or forgiving, bring it out of your mind where you can physically see or audibly sense the emotions.

Processing your thoughts and feelings out loud is a way to take care of yourself physically, mentally, emotionally, and spiritually. By speaking out, you're releasing tension. Venting on paper or with others is useful to unload the distress cooped up within you. You're letting your brain know the threat is leaving or has left. It's satisfying.

Keeping the pressure in is damaging. You can't function optimally when you're chronically withholding your struggles from being known and acknowledged as valid. Fears, worries, and doubts turn into anxiety, panic attacks, and depression when kept hidden. Bottled-up negativity makes it difficult to get good-quality sleep. Unvoiced worries are considered threats by your brain.

You'll keep suffering if the fight, freeze, or flee system is in a perpetually activated mode. Your body needs calm and rest as direly as it requires excitement and movement.

**Not Speaking Out Makes It Difficult for You to Have Restorative Rest and Sleep.**

Have you tried getting good quality sleep when your list of things to do, obligations to meet, issues to address, and other worries flood your mind? It's almost impossible. To cope, you distract or numb yourself with screens, snacks, or alcohol to fall asleep. While your eyes are shut and the conscious part of your brain is temporarily arrested, you're actually not resting and repairing. Food, alcohol, and the blue light emitted by screens consumed within a couple hours of sleeping cause your body to focus on processing these versus resting and repairing.

A good quality sleep is one of the body's primary healing modalities. The National Sleep Foundation defines good quality sleep as the following.

- Sleeping more time while in bed (at least 85 percent of the total time);
- Falling asleep in thirty minutes or less;
- Waking up no more than once per night; and
- Being awake for twenty minutes or less after initially falling asleep.

When you consistently don't get enough good quality sleep, an average of seven to nine hours for adults, your brain accumulates broken cell components that would've been repaired or removed during restorative sleep.

Built up junk gets solidified on the walls of your brain, decreasing the amount of blood that could feed your brain cells oxygen and nutrients. Your brain's executive functioning is compromised. You experience brain fog. You can't think as clearly. It's hard to focus. You make avoidable mistakes. You become easily irritable. Getting things done is harder to do. You lack creative solutions. You forget more often.

When brain junk continues to thicken or a solidified piece breaks off, the brain's highway for blood to pass through gets blocked. Adequate blood volume can't get through, cutting off oxygen and food supply to the brain. As a result, you suffer from detrimental health issues like loss of consciousness, stroke, or internal bleeding. Holding your truth in eventually costs you your life.

You can't distract or numb your way to survive long term or thrive. To overcome, you face and go through hard seasons. So while it feels uncomfortable to do, speak out to process what's in your mind, heart, and gut. When you do, you stack the odds in favor of you getting restorative sleep.

You can release through talking out loud by yourself or praying. You can also speak out with someone who listens well—a coach, mentor, pastor, close friend, or therapist. Engage with a person who's appropriate for what you're looking to process.

The next time you struggle with falling or staying asleep, speak out loud what's bothering you, even when it sounds incoherent. You're not aiming for eloquence. The act of opening up is a win. The more you let out, the better. Hearing out loud what ruminates within allows you to notice your thoughts more clearly.

When thoughts are out in the open, you'll recognize them for what they are. Some are things you thought you care about but actually don't. Others are irrational fears that you can recognize, accept, then decide whether you allow them to take residence in your mind or not. Start with how you're feeling. Let the words flow out of you without judging them. If you sleep next to someone, it's worth getting up and going to a space where you can talk out the contents of your heart and mind without reservation.

In 2020, while quarantined, falling asleep became more difficult than before for many, including myself. I felt tangled in unprocessed thoughts and emotions. Mentally mulling over the state of the world, persisting injustices against human beings, sufferings, death, life as a whole, relationships, finances, health, businesses, and transitioning into a new chapter left me overwhelmed. Speaking out loud my feelings and thoughts helped me work through what's real and addressable and what's outside of my control.

I prefer processing by journaling, praying, and recording voice memos. Yes, problems don't vanish when I acknowledge them. By letting them out, though, I'm able to fall asleep faster and stay asleep throughout the night. Ultimately, you become better equipped to face challenges head-on when your mind and body have sufficient time to recuperate.

For those battling insomnia, I see you. What you're going through is complicated. Speaking out alone won't be sufficient to regain good sleep. It can only be adjunct and complementary to your existing prescribed therapies.

## Detangling Yourself from Worry Is a Form of Speaking Out.

Your feelings of worry are valid. And you're capable of working them out. Silencing or ignoring your worries will only make them come back stronger. Rather than suppressing, notice your concerns. Label them. The act of bringing awareness to what bothers you is healing.

You're unable to distinguish between physical and invisible threats when they're left in your unconscious mind. Whatever danger you sense—real or imagined—your brain triggers the fight, freeze, or flee system. When this system is activated, adrenaline rushes through your body to help you overcome threats. Blood pressure goes up. Heart beats fast. Pupils constrict.

Being in self-preservation mode is necessary for survival. It's helpful when temporary. Your systems do go back to normal.

When you're constantly worried, however, your brain thinks you're perpetually under attack. Your body keeps releasing adrenaline, giving way to chronic systemic inflammation. It can't keep itself tightly regulated. If left unmanaged, chronic diseases like obesity, type 2 diabetes, Alzheimer's, heart and lung diseases, certain cancers, depression, and stroke show up.

By voicing out your worries through art, writing, exercise, or talking about them, you'll be able to release their hold on you. Tucking your worries within keeps you locked in survival mode, but processing them gives you room to thrive. You're worthy of thriving.

## Speaking Out to Set Your Boundaries Is Self-Care.

Managing your energy is key to living a full life. There are people, activities, spaces, and things that bring you vitality and ones that drain your energy. Speaking out to set boundaries is a form of self-care.

Have you ever wondered why you say yes to an ask when you're hesitant to commit? Is it because you're wary of letting others down? What happens when you say yes but then do things haphazardly or quit when the going gets tough? You won't only lose self-confidence in your ability to follow through, you'll also risk putting the other person in a bind.

Your energy must be safeguarded because it's limited. Without enough energy to propel yourself forward, you drift. A life adrift sucks even more energy out of you. You wake up one day in a zombie state: unhappy, unmotivated, unfulfilled, and angry.

Speaking out to set your boundaries isn't selfish. The best way to give to others is when your basic needs are met. You cheerfully serve from a place of overflow rather than deficit. If you're constantly running on empty, you'll risk burnout. Burnout is expensive. It tanks your mood and productivity. It leads to mental and physical states that rob your peace of mind, joy, and life.

To effectively set boundaries, assess and manage your **Capacity-to-Commitment Ratio (C2C)**.

When your C2C is under one, your commitments are greater than your capacity. A little under one is good for growth. When it's over one, your capacity exceeds the demands of your commitments. A little over one is good for healing.

When you're way under a C2C of one, the danger is overextending and burnout. Your commitments are swallowing you whole. You're drowning. When you're way over a C2C of one, there's a risk of boredom and insignificance. You're playing small. You've outgrown your current role and environment.

A C2C best for your well-being is at and around one. In this space, you have enough challenge to stretch you. You're not bored. You're feeling useful. You have margin for the unplanned and inevitable issues. You have room to take advantage of unexpected and purpose-aligned opportunities.

Setting and enforcing your unique boundaries is key to be at and around a C2C of one. Say no even to the good things to be able to deeply focus and create a life you love.

## Other Forms of Self-Care Are a Must for Speaking Out for Yourself.

Having a voice requires grit and stamina. Backlash as a result of speaking out is highly probable. When you physically feel weak and tired, it's tough to stand up for yourself. While speaking out loud to process your truth is a form of self-care, there are other essential strategies to keep your mind, body, and spirit well. In this section, you'll learn select self-care practices to support you in your journey of rediscovering and reclaiming your voice.

**1. Practice Belly Breathing.**

When was the last time you took a deep breath?

When you're not intentional with your breathing, you may not notice when your breathing becomes shallow. Breathing shallow causes your organs and cells to get inadequate oxygen. Insufficient oxygen in cells slows energy production. It traps excess carbon dioxide in, weakening you.

How do you engage your belly when breathing?

I do a box breathing technique. Sit comfortably. Bring your shoulders back and down. Unclench your jaws. Put one hand on top of your belly button. As you inhale through your nose, inflate your belly and feel your hand moving away from your ribs. Do this for a count of four. Then, hold. Keep your hand on your belly steady. Do this for a count of four. When you exhale out your nose, deflate your belly. Feel your hand move toward your ribs. Do this for a count of four. Hold for four. Repeat until you feel slightly light-headed. Your hands can feel tingly. This could be as short or as long as most suitable for you.

Schedule deliberate breathing sessions regularly. You can start with once every other day. You can do it upon waking up as part of a morning routine or when you're powering down at night. You can also use this technique to release tension as needed throughout the day.

## 2. Speak Kindly to Yourself.

Shift your self-talk to one that reinforces a healthy and empowered identity.

Shame, a painful feeling of humiliation, is pervasive in most women's lives. You were taught to doubt your voice. You were told you're too much, too sensitive, or crazy. Negatively labeling behaviors is a maneuver to weaken your resolve to speak your truth.

When you exercise your voice, you activate your power. To resist and persist, speak positively to yourself.

As former United States President Abraham Lincoln stated, "A house divided cannot stand." Similarly, when you're not for you, then how can you keep on keeping on?

Your body is listening to you. You're in charge of it. What you tell yourself dictates how you, on a cellular level, behave. Practice positively affirming yourself.

You're worthy. You matter. You're unconditionally, irrevocably loved. You're enough. You're accepted. You're seen. You're heard. You're beautiful. You're powerful. You're capable. You can grow. You can adapt. You can make things happen. You can start and finish things. You are a Queen.

**3. Incorporate Daily Movement.**

Physicist Isaac Newton's first law of motion states that, "A body at rest will stay at rest and a body in motion stays in motion unless a force acts upon it." Similarly, the way to get out of a slump is to start moving. Yes, the inertia is real. It's hard to start moving your body when you're used to being sedentary. However, more energy gets produced by your body when you're moving than when you're staying in place.

Movement doesn't mean spending countless hours in the gym, lifting weights or running on a treadmill. Those are beneficial yet could be intimidating when you're starting or restarting. Deliberately plan to move your body with an activity that's relatively easy and enjoyable.

To make an activity a habit, James Clear, in his book *Atomic Habits*, suggests to make a task (1) easy, (2) attractive, (3) obvious, and (4) satisfying. There are a myriad of intentional movements that meet these criteria depending on your preference. You can dance, walk the dog, stretch, or practice qigong—an ancient Chinese health method that combines slow, graceful movements with mental concentration and breathing to increase and balance your vital energy.

Pick one activity you can commit to. Schedule it, and track your progress. Focus on finding joy with the practice versus arriving at a set end point. A lifestyle of movement is ever-evolving. There's no finish line.

### 4. Stay Hydrated.

Up to 60 percent of your body is made up of water. Your brain is composed of 73 percent water. When you're not adequately hydrated, your body can't function properly. Water is critical for the brain to create hormones and neurotransmitters that inform your mood, focus, concentration, and more. It helps your body clear up waste. It prolongs the inevitable loss of muscle tone and skin elasticity that come with aging.

For women, about 11.5 cups (1 cup = 8 oz) of fluid a day is recommended by the National Academies of Sciences, Engineering, and Medicine (NASEM). About 20 percent of the daily fluid intake usually comes from food. One rule of thumb I've learned is to drink the ounces of water equivalent to half of your body's weight in pounds. So if you weigh 130 pounds, aim to drink sixty-five ounces of water, or a little over eight cups daily. Listen to your body as you hydrate more. Err on the higher range of recommended water intake.

**5. Increase Your Electrolyte Intake.**

Electrolytes like sodium, calcium, potassium, and magnesium are essential ions the body needs to take in from outside sources. Our bodies are unable to produce them. Most of the time we get enough from food. However, drastic shifts in lifestyle, such as adopting a low-carb diet, intermittent fasting, or sweating profusely can lead to insufficient electrolytes. It's important to pay attention to your electrolyte levels when embarking upon a new nutrition and exercise regimen.

Low sodium and potassium can trigger symptoms such as headaches, muscle cramps, irritability, and lethargy. Low magnesium can lead to muscle cramps, irregular sleep, cognitive issues, and digestive troubles. Low calcium can lead to vitamin D deficiency.

You can consume whole foods to supply your daily calcium (e.g. dairy; dark, leafy vegetables), magnesium (e.g. nuts, seeds, and avocado), and potassium (e.g. banana, spinach, broccoli, mushrooms) needs. Add unrefined mineral salts like sea salt for sodium. Consider dietary supplements if your whole food consumption is inadequate.

### 6. Make Reading a Regular Activity.

The brain is neuroplastic and neuroregenerative. It's capable of change and of rewiring itself. It can generate new brain cells. To support your brain's natural healing and growth abilities, practice regular mental exercises.

Reading is a convenient and relatively easy way to challenge your mind so it can remain flexible. It can also be a form of relaxation. You can choose among fiction or non-fiction books or articles that uplift, educate, or inspire.

Making reading a habit helps you continue to learn long after schooling is done. Becoming a lifelong learner promotes a growth mindset, which is key to a healthy, happy, productive, and meaningful life.

### 7. Be Still.

It's tempting to be busy all the time. The adrenaline that comes from being in a constant rush can be intoxicating. Nonetheless, motion without rest depletes you.

Stillness is key to regain calm and control. Solitude is critical to refresh the mind, body, and soul.

Being still takes time to adopt as a habit. You can

start with a five-minute meditation or breathing exercise, strolling at a relaxed pace, or listening to nature or music. Keeping a stillness practice allows the mind to stay aligned or realign with the rest of the body.

**8. Prioritize Sleep.**

Sleep is key to good health. Insufficient amounts are deleterious to your well-being. Prioritizing sleep will help you get more of it.

Find a schedule you're most likely to stick with on a regular basis. Explore potential barriers and plan for ways to address them. Discuss with the people you live with, if any, when you prefer going to bed. Request for things that can help you keep your sleeping schedule. You can ask for noise to be minimized at a certain hour and for lights to be turned off or dimmed. Arrange for regular activities and engagements to not be scheduled within a couple hours of your bedtime.

Your success in maintaining a sleeping schedule is strongly influenced by the level of support you get. Consider being persistent in protecting your sleep.

**9. Surround Yourself with People Who Make You Feel Loved or Inspired.**

An underrated self-care strategy is carefully choosing the quality of the people in your closest circle. As business mentor Jim Rohn admonished, "You become the average of the five people you hang out with most often." When those you surround yourself with reduce your self-esteem, influence you to settle for less than what you're capable of, or tempt you to dwell in negativity, it's time to re-evaluate your time and energy investments.

Can you lead your pack to spend more time and effort discussing, investing in, or working on things that grow and develop each of you personally and professionally? You may not need to change who you surround yourself with if you can influence the focus of your time together.

If you're closely tied to people who tend to drain your energy regardless of the number of attempts you make to influence their perspective or behavior, consider limiting the topics you discuss and minimizing time spent with them.

Inspiration, learning, and love all lift up the spirit. Make space for these in your life.

**10. Get Some Sunlight.**

Nature—sunlight, water, and trees—is healing and restorative. The more you spend time in it, the more likely you feel well. When you expose your body to sunlight, Vitamin D—protective against inflammation and useful for brain functioning and bone development—is produced. Aim to get it before ten in the morning, and apply sunscreen to reduce exposure to UV rays.

Your health is multidimensional and integrated. One aspect affects the others. Your physical wellness is tied to your mental, emotional, and spiritual health. Warrior Queen, to keep you in the arduous path of rediscovering your voice, it's vital that you make your health a focus.

With this foundation, the next chapters will cover techniques and specific how-to guides on learning and practicing the art of conversation, which is key to effectively speaking out for yourself.

# CHAPTER 6

# Ten Steps to Get Good at Speaking Out for Yourself

**HOW WOULD YOU LIKE** to set yourself up for a future that's healthier and more fulfilling than the life you're living? Deciding to speak out for yourself makes you your own hero. You have all you need to start today.

Speaking out can be intimidating as with anything you do rarely or for the first time. The key to moving forward despite feeling afraid is preparation and practice. Behind bold and articulate individuals are multiple hours of honing their thinking and communication skills.

Don't be disheartened if your first few attempts don't go smoothly or gracefully. It's part of the process. The more you do it, the better and more confident you'll get. Becoming fluent in the art of standing up for yourself takes the repeated practice of utilizing good techniques. Speaking out will eventually feel natural to you.

Here's an example scenario to illustrate:

Anna is in a predicament in deciding what to do with her life after losing her job. She feels torn and confused. She can get another job in healthcare that pays well and is approved by her husband and dad, whom she respects and are close to her. However, she no longer feels challenged or inspired by this line of work. Or, she can go all in on making a living doing what she loves most—watercolor painting.

Anna has role models and mentors who have successfully built digital and product-based businesses, teaching, building a community of, and supplying materials to watercolor enthusiasts. She has no dependents, little student debt, and has no mortgage to pay. She knows success is possible but not guaranteed.

The major downsides she's concerned with starting her own business are (1) not making the six-figure income she's been used to having for years and (2) her husband and dad are discouraging her from pursuing this path full-time. They suggested it stays as her hobby. In her gut, she feels this path is what's right for her at this time of her life.

While she respects her father's and husband's perspectives, she wants to start making career decisions for herself. With much thought and consideration, she finally gives herself permission to go after her dream of making a positive impact in others' lives through watercoloring. Without seeking approval, Anna wants to openly share her decision with her husband and dad.

## Ten Steps to Get Good at Speaking Out for Yourself.

### 1. Think of an optimized objective for the conversation.

An optimized objective focuses your mind on the benefits of speaking out instead of being paralyzed by the dreaded what-ifs. In Anna's case, her concerns include: "What if they get mad and think I'm being reckless and irresponsible?" "What if my thoughts and plans fail and I look stupid?" "What if I'm not ready yet?"

An optimized objective is specific, achievable, and aligned to who you are. It levels your expectations and grounds you.

1. Being specific means choosing an objective that's direct and narrowly focused.
2. An achievable endpoint can be attained within the span of the conversation.
3. An aligned objective is derived from your values and principles.

Some examples of optimized objectives for a conversation are:

- "I'll be clear and decisive in sharing my immediate next steps. I will ask my husband for emotional support and financial support for six months to service my basic needs."
- "I'll share with my manager how I feel about my current compensation package. I'll ask for

a *Y*% raise and give *A, B, C* reasons to support my claim."
- "I'll let him know that his interruptions when I speak in meetings is unacceptable. It makes me feel devalued."
- "I'll remain calm, concise, and respectful as I say no to the offer. I'll thank them for their time and consideration."

In contrast, ineffective objectives can derail you. They're broad, unachievable, and misaligned to who you are.

1. A broad objective dilutes your effectiveness.
2. An unachievable objective isn't realistic for what can be accomplished in one conversation.
3. An unaligned objective focuses on what others would think of you versus what you think of yourself.

Some examples of ineffective objectives for a conversation are:

- "I'll see if they agree with my decision."
- "I'm hoping after I share my weekly updates with my manager, she realizes how hard I work and gives me a raise."
- "I'll put him in his place."
- "I'll share why this position won't work for me so they realize I'm not interested."

## 2. Write down your thoughts and feelings to clarify.

The more you practice expressing yourself on paper, the more comfortable you'll be at seeing your thoughts and feelings out in the open. Your drafts are for your eyes only. Your words will be perfectly imperfect. You'll have to embrace them without judgments as they flow. The objective is to let out what's within you.

Here's an optional starting ritual for the clarifying writing session that follows. It helps expand your mind and get you comfortable with sharing your thoughts. Close your eyes for a few seconds. Breathe in confidence. Exhale out hesitations. Breathe in belief. Exhale out apprehensions. Smile. Feel gratitude. You matter. Your voice matters. Now, write the first things that come to mind when you think of a good day. What would a day look like if you lived it on your own terms? Write it down. How are you feeling at this moment? Write a few words about how you feel.

Let's turn to the subject you want to speak out on. It could be a career move, dealing with finances, relationship and parenting expectations, a new project or venture you want to take on, or hurt you felt with someone's actions or words toward you. Write as many details as you can about your feelings and thoughts on the subject.

What are the pain points you have with your current situation? It could be your reservations on timing, commitment level, effort or resources required, and potential outcomes. It could be that you've been suffering mentally and emotionally due to the situation you want changed. What similar struggles have you already encountered and tolerated? What undesirable impact do you sense coming if you linger with the old?

What excites you about where you're going? What gives you the motivation to face this new path? Who inspires you to dare and be brave? What would your ninety-year-old self think of your decision?

Explore the other party's perspectives. If you thought the way they did, what hesitations and feelings come to mind about you changing courses? What cultural or historical influences could they be referring to as they draw their conclusions? Are these still relevant to how the world operates today? Who would they be if they dared to be themselves? How would they feel about their life if they lived it true to who they are?

The answers to these questions are for you. It's a brain dumping and untangling exercise. You'll want the points you've been considering in your mind to be on paper so you can gain clarity.

When you've exhausted your writing, pause to acknowledge your good work. You may jump to the next step without giving yourself credit for getting this far. It's important to be aware that you've taken a big step by processing your truth. Park your writing for a day and revisit it later to organize your thoughts and choose your main message for the actual conversation.

**3. Organize your thoughts.**

Relax your shoulders and jaws. Shake your limbs. In this step, you'll be organizing and synthesizing the thoughts you wrote in Step 2 to get to your main message. Your aim is to build the ideas one on top of the other in an organized manner so as to keep your audience focused and listening to what you have to say.

There are three ways to structure your thoughts: inverted pyramid, pyramid, and diamond.

1. In the inverted pyramid structure, you start with specific points and later conclude with the big idea.
2. In the pyramid structure, you start with the big idea before sharing the specific points to support the key point.
3. In the diamond structure, you state the big idea, support it with specific points, then conclude with the big idea.

You can experiment on which one applies to your audience, message, and context.

If the main idea is a paradigm shift or is potentially intimidating for your audience, you can choose the inverted pyramid structure. Start with bite-sized information that builds, eventually closing with the main idea.

If you're short on time or the person you're talking to is unable to hold attention for long, a pyramid is the most appropriate. You share the big idea at the outset, and they can choose to process it with the specific points or take it as is without hearing the details.

If you're introducing a new idea to an audience that has some base knowledge or are open to get challenged, like delivering a speech or talk, a diamond structure would be best. You share the point of the talk, back it up with supporting insights, then bring it home by reiterating the big idea.

For situations like Anna's, apply the inverted pyramid structure. Start with how you feel about your career experiences and trajectory. Share what has been most interesting and enlightening and what has been depleting and discouraging. Close with stating your decision, what you hope to do next, and what support can look like from your loved ones.

Review what you wrote on Step 2 and organize your thoughts using the following guide.

a. What's the one takeaway you'd like your audience to leave with after this one conversation?
b. What ideas, insights, or thoughts can help them see this main idea?

   c. Which structure would work best for the context and what you know about the receiver of your message (inverted pyramid, pyramid, or diamond)?

**4. Edit your text to make it concise.**

Editing gives your message the refining it needs to be at its most potent form. Your words are like a double-edged sword. To sharpen it requires grinding against a hard surface. Similarly, grind out the excess to make your words most impactful.

The objective with this step is to deliver the one main idea you've organized in Step 3 in the fewest words possible without losing meaning. Every point you'll be sharing builds the one main idea. The desired outcome is a cohesive and concise statement that keeps the emotions you want to convey intact. Choose your words with intention without sounding like a robot.

To begin editing, think of your audience as a fifth grader. You want to use everyday, conversational language. Keep one thought per sentence. Complex sentences create confusion, especially when emotions run high. Simple and straightforward sentences bring clarity. When going over your text, see what words you can eliminate or replace while keeping the meaning.

**5. Record yourself when practicing.**

For self-feedback, record your voice as you practice. Practice as if you're talking to your intended listener.

Read out loud your edited message. This serves as your guide and outline as you practice. It's not intended as a script to be memorized.

Your voice carries your message. There's a version of your voice that commands and maintains attention. It's your chest voice. A chest voice is characterized by low pitch and a deep, warm tone. In contrast, your head voice is high pitched. To get to your lower register, inhale deeply through your nose and exhale from your belly as you speak.

In Julian Treasure's TED Talk, "How to speak so that people want to listen," he shared six ways to warm up your voice in preparation for an important conversation. I found these helpful to do. For the first step, Treasure recommends raising your hands, taking a deep breath in, and exhaling with a sigh. To warm up the lips, repeat the word "buh" a few times. Then, trill your lips. To warm up the tongue, repeat an exaggerated "la" sound. Then, roll an R. Lastly, make a "wee-awh" sound where the "wee" is high-pitched and "awh" is low-pitched.

In addition to tone and voice warm-ups, pacing, enunciation, and volume are key components of an engaging voice. Practice a slower pace when speaking. Most times, you lean toward talking fast when nervous. Allow pauses and silence. You don't have to talk nonstop. Often, filling the silence is your way to avoid getting interrupted. It's okay. You can pause.

To enunciate your words without being overly done, catch the last syllable of each word. It helps the listener hear your words clearly.

If you tend to speak softly, practice speaking progressively louder without shouting. Belly breathing helps give your voice power. Engage your core as you exhale and speak.

While these basics can be sufficient to improve your voice quality for overall message impact, you can further hone it with a speaking voice coach.

**6. Do a mock conversation with a trusted person.**

Having one or more mock conversations with a trusted person after you've prepared is a good way to work through your nervousness. Hours before I was giving a talk on "The Power of Empathy in Innovation" to the top 200 executives of the largest healthcare company in the world, I did a dry run of my well-rehearsed speech on stage. I wasn't sure if it was the lighting or being hooked up with a mic, but I froze midway through. My fears came to life. The audio executive asked if I wanted to redo it, and I sheepishly said, "Yes, please." The second mock talk went smoothly. And I delivered what the audience later told me was a powerful and inspiring message.

Do a trial run for your important conversations even when you're not speaking on stage. You can be in your kitchen with your spouse, a meeting room with your boss or colleagues, or a playground with another parent and still freeze from fear. Succeeding in mock conversations will give you a big boost of confidence to boldly execute the real one.

Request your enlisted confidante to play the role of your target audience. Let them know how important the conversation is to you and what's at stake. Share with them your optimized objective so they have the context needed to help you polish your delivery. Then, give them permission to give you feedback as appropriate to get you ready for the real talk.

Know that while you may trip and not do as well as you hoped during the mock conversation, you're still learning and improving. Stay encouraged. Believe in yourself.

### 7. Anticipate how your audience may push back.

If there was a magic wand to wave and remove all likelihood that the person you'll be speaking out to will not have some pushback, I'd give it to you. But it doesn't exist. You'll more than likely encounter resistance. Believe that you're capable of facing it head-on and standing firm.

Anticipating their likely rebuttal will help you feel calm during the conversation. Of course, the other person can throw a curveball you won't see coming. That's okay. Preparing for some is better than not preparing for any.

You can learn a few techniques from boxing that can be applied to speaking out for yourself. There are offensive moves where you jab, cross, hook, or throw an uppercut. Equally important is learning to use defensive moves like bobbing, weaving, blocking, and slipping. Practicing both types of moves is key to increase your chances of fighting for yourself well.

Based on what you know about the person, what are the likely things they could tell you that could make you feel self-conscious? What buttons could they press? What would be a trigger they pull that could make you lose control over your emotions? Write these down.

Before the conversation, check in with yourself. How could you reframe the other person's words so you stay focused on your optimized objective? What would you keep in mind when you start to feel self-doubt, fear, or worry? What would be your exit strategy if you felt cornered?

If you were Anna, what would you keep in mind if they reply, "That's careless. You're self-sabotaging. Are you crazy?" when you push back against their recommendation? What would you say or do if they continue to resist after sharing your truth?

You may have the tendency to feel defensive and turn to berating to protect yourself. Or you may close up and stonewall. Instead of reacting, predetermine a countermove that will make you proud of yourself.

Pause when you feel your heart starts beating erratically. Breathe deeply. Allow silence to enter the chat.

Words don't need to fill every second of the conversation. Remember why you are speaking out for yourself. Recall your optimized objective. Slow your speech when you respond. Aim for direct and concise response.

You can say, "I hear you. Thank you for letting me know your perspective. But I need to do what's right for me. I hope you can support my decision." They may not immediately give in to your request for support. Would you be okay with that? Discomfort is okay. It's what growth entails. Being true to who you are is essential to living a life with no regrets.

### 8. Schedule a time for the conversation.

There is an opportune time of day for a challenging conversation to happen. This is usually when you and your audience are least stressed and most rested. Yet the perfect timing doesn't exist.

It's better to schedule something earlier rather than wait for a perfect time. Waiting too long may cause you to talk yourself out of speaking out. Remember that your brain would prefer comfort over challenge. The longer you wait to speak out, the more likely you'll keep silent. On the other hand, jumping to talk while experiencing heightened emotions may cause you to lose your cool, behave and say things in ways you'd regret later, or force your audience to dialogue when they're not ready to converse.

A good rule of thumb is speaking when you still feel some uneasiness but not at a point when you're distraught. At the same time, check in with your audience to make sure they're not overly distracted or exhausted when you engage them in a crucial chat. If you choose to wait until you're fully calm without jitters, it may not happen. Feeling nervous or antsy is okay, but speaking out of intense feelings may cause a huge backfire.

What gets scheduled is highly likely to get done. To ensure that the conversation does take place, look to schedule a time to talk with your target audience. You may find it difficult to find a time when you and they are in the best mood—fully rested, happy, and full. Refrain from pressuring yourself to find a perfect time. There may not be one. Look for the next best open time instead. Are they more likely to be in a generally okay mood at night after dinner? Schedule your tough talk then. Are they morning people and prefer to tackle hard things first thing in the day? Make your appointment with them then. What you are aiming for is finding an okay time—not necessarily the most prime one because that time may not come.

### 9. Execute.

The steps that led you to this stage were all part of the preparation. They make up 80 percent of the process for a reason. Preparing your mind, voice, and message is key to succeed in speaking out. Yet none of the preparation and practice will mean anything unless you actually do the talk. This step is simple and it's the hardest.

Take a deep breath. Let's run through a condensed version of what you've been practicing. Visualize the positive outcome you desire. Feel relieved. Feel alive. Feel empowered. Feel bold. Sense your power welling within and then coming out of you fully. Know you are worthy. Your voice matters. Your feelings are valid. You make sense. Shut out the noise. Momentarily block the fears. Suspend self-criticism and doubts. Then, calmly let out the words. Let them roll out of you as rays of sunshine burst through grey clouds.

Speak slower than normal. Catch the last syllable of your words. Embrace pauses. Let silence ring when it comes, as it inevitably will. Say what's on your mind. Share what you feel. Breathe. Blink. It's done.

You did it.

**10. Celebrate you for speaking out.**

Regardless of the reaction and response from your audience, you've done what's good for and true to yourself. You let your thoughts and feelings be known. You gave yourself permission to speak out for yourself. You're your own champion. Well done, Queen. Take in the power of standing firmly. You took up space. Congratulations.

Done is a gift that keeps giving. Your execution gives precedence for your mind to follow in the future. You are paving a new pattern for yourself. You spoke out. You will continue to speak out. As you make this a habit, you open yourself to a new identity. This identity says you are unapologetic about yourself. You accept yourself for who you are. You reveal your inner life because you matter. You're not invisible. You are seen. You are heard. You did this. You will keep on keeping on.

## PRACTICE SCENARIOS

You may have picked up this book without a specific situation to speak out about. Maybe you've already completed tackling one situation requiring you to say what's on your mind. Still, you long to put the techniques to action and practice so you can hone this life skill for future needs. Here are a couple of major scenarios where you can practice the above steps.

**1. Practice saying no to things that don't make you come alive.**

As a popular saying goes, "If it's not a heck yes, it's a heck no." Have you always gone with the flow? Have you often conceded with what others, especially those in authority, required or asked of you? Some of those things may have been positive and healthy. Some may have left you feeling disrespected, disempowered, or regretful.

Saying no is a difficult task. But you'll get more comfortable the more you do it. To get started, here are a few clutch phrases you can use. Practice saying them with confidence in the mirror. Look yourself in the eye and say them out loud. It may feel silly at the beginning. What you're doing is training your mind to remember these phrases. They may come in handy when you're caught off guard and need to spontaneously speak out or risk keeping quiet against what's best for you.

- "This won't work for me."
- "This isn't working."
- "That made me feel uncomfortable."
- "I'm not okay with that."
- "That's unacceptable."
- "I don't want it at this time or with these conditions."
- "I'll pass on this one."
- "That's inappropriate."
- "I'm okay without it."
- "This is not a good time."
- "Stop."
- "No."

**2. Practice saying yes to things that can grow you.**

When you've gone through many past hardships and trauma, you tend to hang around your comfort zone indefinitely. You can't blame yourself. Life's been tough. What you've been through is no joke. Stability and predictability feel safe and secure. I hear you. At some point, though, you will need to teeter beyond what's familiar and comfortable to keep growing.

Steady-state is transient.

No one should tell you when and how to be. And you can consider saying yes to things that can grow you. Do it with ease by starting small. Take pauses along the way. With consistent pursuit of progress, you'll become more open to embracing challenges. The nerves and uneasiness won't go away. Yet you'll be more likely to do hard things even when you feel queasy or afraid.

Only you can determine what will be challenging for you. Gain self-awareness by reflecting on where you are in the spectrum of the following well-being areas.

- **Exercise:** Do I vigorously move my body every day and need to add the discipline of rest and recovery? Or am I more frequently sedentary and need to add the discipline of movement?
- **Nutrition:** Am I too conscious of what I eat and can use embracing freedom from guilt? Or am I mindless when it comes to snacking or eating and can push myself to be more intentional?
- **Work:** Am I working nonstop and can schedule more downtime to rest, explore, and be still? Or am I doing work less than what I am capable of and can seek more challenging projects?
- **Relationships:** Am I pouring and leaving my soul empty to make a partnership work and can benefit from creating space for self-care? Or am I

more focused on my needs and can do more for others?
- **Finances:** Do I spend more than I save and can benefit from adding structure to where my money goes? Or do I save more than I spend and can make room to give in to some micro indulgences?
- **Spiritual:** Do I go through life unconscious of my purpose and can invest attention in exploring and aligning how I spend my time in pursuit of a mission bigger than me? Or do I go through life obsessed with only doing what I believe is my purpose and can flex my trust muscles during a waiting season or welcome the unplanned and unexpected detours?

To practice saying yes more often to things that can expand you, here are some phrases to prime your day. Practice saying them out loud within the first hour of waking up.

- *Yes, I can.*
- *Yes, I will.*
- *Yes, I must.*
- *Yes, I trust.*
- *Yes, I am.*

Practice increases the chances you'll arrive at your intended destination. Practicing helpful techniques discussed here will set you up to feel more confident in speaking out for yourself. Nonetheless, practice doesn't guarantee you'll always get what you hoped for or worked toward. Remember that how others react to you speaking out is outside your circle of control.

You're only responsible for the input not the output. Accept what comes your way with lots of grace and kindness for yourself. Speaking out is for the brave. It's not easy, which is why many years have gone by without you doing it. Remember that you have what it takes to keep on speaking out your truth.

Now, you'll need your own people. Having a tribe where speaking out is a norm will make this journey a lot more doable for you. In the next chapter, we'll be exploring details on why, how, where, and what to keep in mind when looking for your people.

# PART THREE:

## Be As You Are

# CHAPTER 7
## Find Your Own People

**YOU WEREN'T MEANT TO HEAL AND GROW ALONE.** You were meant to do life with others. And not everyone is your people. Some will like and celebrate you. Others won't.

It's not your fault when select people don't accept and embrace you for who you are. You have to find those who are for you at each stage of your life.

Have a diverse support tribe. You need at least one who challenges you without violating your boundaries. It's vital to have one who loves you unconditionally. And it's necessary to have one who holds space for you to feel the highs and the lows without trying to fix anything.

Stop settling for those who are conveniently in your life right now. Just because they've been with you for a long time doesn't mean they should be with you going forward. Assess what you need and don't need.

Evaluate how the people closest to you are impacting you. Are they being honest, truthful, kind, considerate, and compassionate? Do they act with your best interest in mind? Do they challenge you without shaming? Do they treat you with respect for your human dignity? Share what you feel and suggest changes in attitude and behavior. However, don't put the burden of changing people on you. Only they can change their own selves.

Be relentless in curating the people you keep close to you. You're not being picky without cause. You're exercising your discernment so you don't only survive life but thrive living it.

When it comes to family members or coworkers who are displaying unhealthy behaviors, it may be harder to distance yourself, yet it's still possible. You can minimize the time and attention you give to those who aren't conducive to your safety, wellness, and progress. You can choose the topics you discuss with them.

You amplify or dampen the quality of your life based on the norms of the people around you. This chapter is about understanding the importance of having people who speak out for themselves more often than not. It's also about knowing who your people are, how to find and engage with them, and what to do in seasons when you're yet to be with those who bring out your unique voice.

## Mirroring the Norm Is How You Learned to Behave.

You have mirror neurons in your brain. Mirror neurons are the cells that help you learn how to behave in the world by copying what the majority around you does. You learned most through mimicking.

When you were a baby and as you grew up, you mirrored the ones who took care of you and whose approval mattered to you. You adopted their mannerisms, tone of voice, and views about the world and your place in it. This training formed the foundation of your behavior and, subsequently, your perceived identity.

You may have observed your mother or father repeatedly stay quiet when there were disagreements. They talked about their issues only after they compounded. Your brain logged this behavior as the norm that you copy when faced with a similar situation. You stay silent in the face of contention until it becomes too much to contain. Then, you implode or explode.

You may have seen other adults in your life retract their words when questioned or challenged. Most people around you behaved this way, so you followed in their steps. You may have learned to deny yourself things you wanted but seemed out of reach. Instead of advocating for yourself and finding a way to get them, you dismissed your desires and let go without persevering.

What you most often mimicked became your go-to action. Your go-to actions repeated over time created your current pattern of behavior, habits, and tendencies. People tend to keep doing what they've repeatedly copied others doing. This is how humans learned to walk, talk, read, write, and navigate the world.

Having built-in reactions learned from others is the way humans survive. You don't have to figure out everything on your own. It's easier for the brain to copy and store behaviors as shortcuts than to keep starting from scratch. Because of the shortcuts, your brain isn't overwhelmed processing each thing you face during the course of a day.

Are all these shortcuts useful forever? No. As software needs updating, so do you. You're not stuck with an existing formatting. You can rewrite your patterns.

Yes, it will be difficult and time-consuming to unlearn and relearn habits. And it's possible. In recent history, scientists have discovered that the human brain is malleable. It can grow, make new cells, and recreate new pathways. It doesn't happen at once. It takes intention and repetition for new ways of being to be your default setting.

When you become aware that many of your patterns come from mirroring others' habits, you gain a powerful perspective. What you do with that awareness will determine how you live your life. Will you accept that those closest to you affect your quality of life and therefore be mindful of who gets to be with you? Or will you deny the influence of your environment and stay in the cycle you've been in? The choice is yours to make.

## You Can Join Circles with Established Norms That Align with Behaviors You Want to Adopt.

Because of mirroring, it takes more effort and persistence to go against the grain than with it. You either become who you're closest to or spend a lot of time and effort resisting norms.

An alternative path is to join a different circle with an existing way of life similar to what you aspire to live. You do this in real life by increasing the distance between you and those whose lifestyle you want to avoid. Concurrently, increase proximity with the ones you want to emulate.

If you want to speak out more, get closer to those who already do. This way makes your progress far more likely to continue and stick than not.

## Who Supports You on This Journey of Rediscovering Your Voice?

The ones who support you during this season of training yourself to speak out more aren't afraid to give you constructive feedback when appropriate. At the same time, they give you space and support so you can make things happen for yourself and offer grace when you fall short of your goals. Around them, you feel safe to speak out without fear of being gossiped about, shamed, or put down.

The real ones aren't those who talk highly but demonstrate poorly. Rather, they're the ones who think, breathe, and live with integrity. In their process, they inspire and encourage. Of course, they'll have flaws. Nonetheless, they grow and learn from their mistakes.

Look for the ones who take ownership and accountability for their limitations and capitalize on their strengths. They're the ones who make no excuses when they fail and don't throw a pity party. Find the ones who are unafraid to be wrong when they speak out. At the same time, they're good at listening and know when to let silence ring. Seek the ones who mind their words but don't focus on what others say about them.

Stay close to those who ask good questions that expand and shift your perspective. They're also open to be challenged without acting defensive. You'll know your tribe by their fruits. How do others feel and behave around them and without their presence? Is there respect and integrity, honor and freedom, accountability without judgment, calm and growth, grace and challenge? If so, these are your people.

**Keep Your Distance from People Who Make You Feel Small.**

Others will cause you to shrink only when you let them. Keep a safe distance away from those who belittle you. If you're not able to do it immediately, start plotting for and get support to eventually get freed. Being belittled will make you want to be silent and conceal your thoughts and feelings. It's toxic to your sanity and a deterrent to your healing and progress.

First, they make you feel small. They do this by interrupting you when you talk, dismissing your opinions as invalid, stupid, or crazy, and inserting doubt by asking, "How can you be so sure?" Feeling small will cause you to doubt your voice. You seek validation and permission with each thought, feeling, and decision. Eventually you stop trusting yourself. Nothing you do feels right until someone else assures you of it. You begin to believe the lie that if no one approves, then it must not be right. When you do this over time, you lose your power of voice and the ability to choose and pursue what's best for you when it's against the norm.

The belittler's intentions may not be to harm you. They think they're keeping you safe by putting you in a box. However, their ignorance of the impact of their words and actions toward you isn't an excuse for their behavior to be tolerated. You must call them out. If they refuse to confront their issues and make strides to do better, it's not your responsibility to fix them. Shake off the dust from your feet and move on. You must find your own way and make decisions for your own self. It starts by voicing out your truth regardless of whether others agree or disagree.

When people have yet to accept, process, and heal from past traumas, they cause others to shrink with them. It's a defense mechanism. They find others who are hurting and not yet mending and keep them from healing.

Temporarily pulling others down allows them to survive in the short-term. However, staying in this state over the long-term keeps them trapped in a victim and blaming mindset. Then, they spiral down, perpetually losing power over their own destinies. They hurt others as they drag them down. If you stay close, you'll drown with them.

It's not your business to save others. You can throw a lifeboat, but you're not the lifeboat. They have to choose to get on the path of healing. Many stay wounded because having open wounds has become familiar. What's familiar feels safe and comfortable. Healing represents change. And change is intimidating and scary even if it's the path to freedom and glory.

Speaking out is a foundational step to get out of a sinking state. When you share out loud your thoughts and feelings, you give your mind the opportunity to decide. Which thoughts and feelings stay with you and get acted upon? Which ones are noticed, then released? By speaking out, you're signaling to yourself that you matter. Your unique perspective isn't to be hidden but to be brought out into the light.

**Get as Close as Possible to the Ones Who**

**Make It Safe for You to Share Your Truth.**

Reflect on the people around you. Are you surrounded with brave, bold, and beautiful people who are unapologetically themselves while making room for you to be you? When you're in their presence, do you feel accepted and empowered? Do they make you feel seen, heard, and known?

My close friend Fatimah Williams has this impact on me. Whenever we get together, I can reveal my limitations, areas of confusions, and big, audacious dreams. Her presence makes me feel bold and unencumbered. I'm certain she's not perfect, yet her on-point perspective and timing of silence seem to be her areas of strength. It doesn't matter what time zone difference is between us, she continues to inspire me to be all that I am and speak out my mind.

A couple of years ago, we connected weekly for three months while I was on an international business assignment in China and she was in New Jersey. Despite the physical distance, her empathy and wisdom traversed and reached the depths of my soul and mind anyway. She's my soul sister and peer mentor. I'm grateful for her being in my life.

Similarly, without feeling judged, my sister Micah Rose welcomes the expression of my thoughts and feelings. I have a habit of kneeling, crying, and praying when I feel overwhelmingly grateful, afraid, or victorious. I primarily do this in my private abode, during my personal quiet time. Yet on many occasions when I visited my sister in her home, she has caught me in the middle of several of these personal speaking-out sessions. At first I was embarrassed. But her reassuring words, "Do what you need to do, Ate (Filipino term for older sister)," helped me accept my own form of sharing my mind out loud.

You don't have to have twenty people who serve this role in your life. You only need a few solid ones to drastically improve your ability and practice of speaking out for yourself. Below are the top qualities to look for in your people.

**1. They accept themselves for who they are.**

People who own their strengths as well as their weaknesses extend this acceptance toward others. They're less likely to put people down or pressure others who aren't doing well. Being surrounded by self-accepting people feels uplifting. There's an undertone of grace. There's an understanding that people are works-in-progress regardless of the level of their achievements in life and work.

**2. They believe in investing in personal growth.**

Being around people who make personal growth a priority is motivating. These are ones who walk the talk and are not merely thinking about growth. They get the nonlinear, intentional journey of becoming better than how you were yesterday.

Some days you see progress. Other days it feels like you've retracted several steps. There are seasons when it feels like you've found flow and are merrily cruising forward despite the inherent discomfort. Then there are stages when growth feels like a steep, uphill climb where you don't see past the next step, and you doubt whether you have what it takes to proceed.

Speaking out for yourself is a personal growth endeavor. It follows the same up and down trajectory as other growth goals. Those who invest in personal growth will understand and support you in this quest.

**3. They embrace that feelings are valid and they hold space for you to process your thoughts.**

Humans feel. That's an indelible part of being human. Those that shun expression of feelings will make it difficult for you to accept your feelings as valid. Those that accept that you're okay with however you feel will make you more likely to confront and let out your emotions.

They don't necessarily have to agree with you, but they will hold space for you to release your pent-up thoughts and feelings. They'll ask you open questions to help you untangle what's within. They're not looking or acting like they are there to fix what you're going through. Nonetheless, their presence is an immense gift.

## Put Yourself Out There.

As of the writing of this book, no one could yet read another person's mind. This is why it's paramount for you to risk putting your thoughts and feelings out there in order to find your people who can keep encouraging and supporting you to speak out your truth.

It takes speaking out to keep speaking out. At first you may start small and with a few people. Then you can gradually increase the frequency of communication and breadth of subjects disclosed.

Even with those closest to you from birth, like your siblings or parents, you may not know if they're a good fit for you unless you test the waters through disclosure of what you think and feel. At this point, you can discern whether you feel valued and supported as you reveal a bit of what you're going through.

My sister wasn't always the person who helped me become more open. However, life experiences matured her. And as she found more of herself, she became the trusted confidante who helps me be more outspoken, communicative of my thoughts and feelings, and transparent. It took me testing the waters periodically to determine if she could be my person.

I didn't meet Fatimah until my late twenties. A pastor friend of ours made the connection. Had we not risked being vulnerable with each other, deeper each time, we may not have developed the friendship and mentorship we now enjoy. It took years of building trust through deliberate connections—talking, listening, and sharing life.

You can't expect to find your people by isolating yourself from others. A good fit between two people can only be discovered up close and personal. Yes, it's scary. You'll get rejected and suffer through bad tries before you find those that will make all the failed attempts worth it.

Press on in finding your people.

## Be Patient with Yourself as You Search and Wait to Find Your People.

Searching for your people can feel frustrating and lonely. There will be days when you'll be tempted to go back to the ones who were easily accessible yet you know aren't right for your healing and growth. Put up protective measures and accountability so you avoid reverting to being with people who treat you badly. These measures could include unfollowing them on social media, deleting and blocking their contact information, and avoiding circles and places that increase the likelihood of you encountering them.

Be kind to and patient with yourself. Only you will be with you for as long as you live on earth. Accept that the process of finding those who are conducive for your speaking out for yourself takes time. Listen to your body. There will be days when you won't feel motivated to put yourself out there. You're okay. There will be days when it will feel uncertain whether you'll be comfortable advocating for your needs and wants. This is normal, and it will pass.

As you wait to meet your people, exercise faith. Believe in yourself. Believe in something bigger than yourself. If you believe in God, remember that His plans are for you and not against you. Stay the course. Preach truth to yourself. You matter. Your voice is power. You have what you need to overcome your old patterns. You can find your people who already speak out their truth and will make it easier for you to do so. They will come.

Refuse to force connections to happen. Who is meant for you will make you feel valued, accepted, and celebrated. Be at peace knowing that as you make deliberate efforts to connect with others and get to know yourself better, you will, in time, attract those who are for you.

# CHAPTER 8

# Pick Your Battles to Get Smart About Speaking Out

IF EVERYTHING IS A PRIORITY, THEN NOTHING IS. The same goes for what you speak out on. Just because you can speak out on everything doesn't mean you should. Speaking out takes effort. It's a risk when it's done. For relatively low-risk topics like choosing what to wear, eat, or have as a hobby, you can speak out often. For high-stake topics where you encounter disagreements, be selective on what you speak out on. High-stakes areas include choosing where to live, what career to pursue, who to have as your life or business partner, advocating for a promotion, raise, or role expansion at work, and how to manage finances and parenting. Not everything is worth championing. But some things are worth risking your time, energy, and social capital to fight for.

## Speaking Out Without Listening Will Dilute Your Effectiveness.

To influence others, they must feel like they can influence you too. You can demonstrate your ability to be influenced by acknowledging others' opinions and suggestions. It doesn't mean you agree with what they say. It means you honor and respect their thoughts and feelings as valid even when you oppose them. Respect and opposition aren't mutually exclusive. You can respect another person with differing points of view while valuing your own stance on the matter.

To indicate that you're listening, you can mirror their statements by repeating what they said. When you mean it, the following statements can make the other person feel like they are getting through to you. "So you are saying (insert what they said)?" "And by that you meant, (insert your interpretation of what they said)?" Allowing others to clarify themselves and being perceived accurately makes them feel valued and known. This increases your level of influence in their lives.

When you think of a response while the other is still expressing their thoughts, you lose touch with the present moment. Anything you say after will come across as disingenuous and self-serving. Why would someone hear you out when you don't also hear them out? Leadership expert and author Stephen Covey aptly summarizes this principle: "Seek first to understand then be understood." I challenge you to listen carefully when others speak their mind and see how often you get reciprocated. Of course, not everyone will hear you even when you hear them. However, more often than not, others respond positively to those who give them a fair chance to speak out.

If you speak out without listening, you will be perceived as close-minded and stubborn. Also, your effectiveness when speaking out will drop drastically. I used to be this way. It was rooted in fear of not being able to finish my thoughts and getting interrupted. I told myself, "If I speak nonstop, then I can get what I'm thinking all out, uninterrupted." At first I was unaware of the impact. I thought that because my intention wasn't bad, my actions would be appropriate. But intention doesn't equate to impact. You can be well-intentioned and still hurt your chances of attaining your goal. For one-time negotiations, I won most of the time. I spoke out until others got exhausted and gave up. But for long-term relationships, I won at first but lost in the end.

In my quest to increase my effectiveness in making things happen through speaking out, I took a step back and reflected. I observed effective individuals and leaders who seemed to have a high rate of success in engaging others to ride with their vision long term. When they spoke, people listened. And it wasn't always the ones in positions of authority. There were people in authority who received nods from their team, but when they left the room, no one on the team followed through with what the boss suggested. Then there were ones who weren't in a position of authority but had command of the team. I sought to learn the root cause of the difference in the impact of these two types of people.

What I found is that effective leaders and those happy in long-term relationships welcomed oppositions and listened without formulating a comeback. They didn't always get their way. Nonetheless, on areas that mattered most to them, their viewpoints were thoroughly considered. They consistently put a stake in the ground only on a few. For the rest of the time, they created space for others to speak their mind. When they did rally for something, others listened and rallied behind them.

## Speaking Out on Everything Will Drain You.

The greater the size of the resistance, the more energy it requires to overcome. Similarly, the higher the number of resistance, the more energy they require to overcome. Every morning, you have a set amount of energy that can sustain you for the day. Some days you are brimming with force. You feel unstoppable. On other days, you're dragging yourself out of bed. This is normal and expected. You're not divine in that you don't run out of energy. You're human; your energy is capped for the day. It ebbs and flows depending on the season you're in.

If by noon you've already spoken out a multitude of times, your remaining energy for the rest of the day will be lower than what you had within an hour of waking up. When evening rolls around and you have a critical conversation, you're likely not going to have the mental clarity, energy, or patience to deliver your thoughts and feelings and listen well.

Every conversation you speak out on takes force out of you. You give out energy when you speak out. Those conversations where you're advocating for your dissenting opinion deplete you. When you're a beginner in speaking out, you're more likely to get worn out with each episode than when it has become a habit.

## Speaking Out Without Sometimes Giving in Will Push Others Away.

Know someone who seems to pick a fight on everything? They hardly concede. What label do they get with people around them? More than likely, they're perceived as combative and disagreeable. Are you clear on what absolutely matters to them? You can't pinpoint exactly what's important. Thus, your defenses are up when you engage. You can't seem to get through, so your default is to oppose them often. Speaking out doesn't mean lashing out. It also doesn't mean getting your way every time.

Human relations and life are complicated. You get to be heard when you speak out and listen. You get to have what you want when you ask for what you don't have and share what you have. When you only get without giving, soon you only give without getting. Life and relationships are giant meshes of pushes and pulls. To win the war, you must concede some battles. To live a life you want, you must make some sacrifices.

It takes something valuable to make something valuable. For speaking out to bring out the best in you and bring in good people in your life, you must learn to give up control sometimes. You can't be right all the time. It can't always be your way or nothing.

Speaking out without giving in drives others away because it feels like the relationship is a one-way versus two-way channel. Without compromise, others pull away from you because they don't feel included. While you're free, others won't feel free in a relationship where only you get to say your truth and not them.

Speaking out and compromise can both be part of your daily life. You can say your truth while letting others win as well. When you do both, you're more likely to attract and keep the people for you while repelling the ones who aren't for you.

## Being Intentional Makes You Selective on

## When and What to Speak Out On.

I was driving home on a one-lane road behind a Tesla driver going as low as ten miles per hour below the speed limit. When the road finally had two lanes, I, in my Nissan Versa, overtook the Tesla. In my peripheral vision, I noticed the driver fiddling with the GPS. That moment taught me a crucial lesson on being intentional. When you don't know where you're going, it doesn't matter how powerful the vehicle you drive. You're bound to go slow.

A clear intention sharpens your focus and makes you go faster, more safely.

Where are you going when you speak out for yourself? Do you know? Knowing your intentions will make you speak out more selectively. Being intentional means you are clear when, how, how often, on what topics, and with whom you speak out to. When you get specific, you get selective.

A shotgun approach to speaking out is the least effective and is the most likely method that backfires on you. When you shoot with a shotgun, you don't only hit your target; you also damage a large area around it. The job doesn't get done cleanly. It leaves a huge mess. In contrast, a sniper approach to speaking out gets work done with the least undesirable effects. When you're intentional, you apply a sniper approach. Your laser-focus pays off in respect and credibility. People trust those who get things done without too many side effects. When your message and delivery tend to be pointed, you're more likely to get to your desired endpoint without too much collateral damage.

### Knowing What You're Willing to Walk Away from Makes You Selective on When and What to Speak Out On.

When you don't know what you're okay losing, you'll think everything has to be won. When you think everything needs to be won, you'll exhaust yourself fighting and miss out on what will actually make you happy and peaceful in the long term. You'll spend your limited capital in your capped time on earth speaking out on things that don't materially add up goodness in your life.

Take a moment and reflect. Are you okay letting others have the last say? What subjects are you willing to not be the expert on? In what areas can you accept not being right?

It takes less effort defining your dislikes than your absolute loves. It's easier to know what you're okay not having than locking in on what you must have. It takes a shorter time determining what to reject than what to accept.

So if honing in your target feels overwhelming, start identifying the areas you can chip off. Like Michelangelo, you'll reveal your equivalent of David by carving out the marble you can forgo. This doesn't make the chipped-off marble less inherently valuable. However, for your specific purposes, those you walk away from don't matter as much as seeing your vision to life.

## Having Self-Awareness Makes You Selective on When and What to Speak Out On.

Knowing yourself is a lifelong process. It has no ending. You keep becoming as long as you're breathing. And the more you know who you are, the more you get good at choosing what to fight for and what to let go of.

To gain self-awareness, you need to be present. To be more present, you need to cut distractions. Avoid multitasking. Do one thing in a given period before moving on to doing another thing. When you concentrate on tackling one task at a time, you're more likely to catch and retain the different reactions that arise within you for every stimulus you encounter. Often, you don't know what to speak out on because you don't know enough about who you are.

What triggers what responses—good, bad, and ugly—from you? They are signals to learning more about yourself. What inspires you? What puts you in a foul mood? What brings you calm? What makes you feel flustered? What makes you come alive? What kills your soul? What do you do that flows naturally to you? What activities make you feel like you are pushing against a boulder up a steep climb? Make mental and written notes about these. They inform your current inclinations, which change over time and contexts.

When you know more about you, you let more things slide while being firmer on championing for a select few.

## Reading the Room Makes You Selective on

## When and What to Speak Out On.

You can know more about yourself while still remaining oblivious to your surroundings. To further tune up your ability to select your timing when speaking out, pay attention to your surroundings. Your best asset here is your observational skills. Similar to getting to know you better, you become more attuned to your environment and others in it when you focus.

Observe one person and behavior at a time before moving on to the next.

I got better at timing when to speak out when I became more keen at observing others' non-verbal gestures. You learn more about what a person believes and feels about something by their behavior, tone of voice, and what they don't say more than what they do say.

A pivotal point in my corporate career happened early for me—during my third summer internship at a Fortune 50 company. I had a massive project. It was one that the sponsoring director informed me later he was hesitant to give to an intern. It would lead to defining a future of an established brand. The project team was at a gridlock situation. More than half of the team were more than willing to go forward with investing millions in one direction while a few critical members were solidly against sinking in more resources. Instead of "faking it until I made it," I spent the first two weeks watching and making notes of how each member of the team behaved during our project meetings and my one-on-one sessions with them. I risked making a weak first impression in favor of having an undisrupted opportunity to learn more about my teammates. At the same time, I studied the data and made initial hypotheses.

After my observational period, I started speaking out. I knew when to talk to make an impact, when to strategically interrupt, and when to pause and keep quiet. How did I know? I learned by observation. I noticed what behaviors steered the team in which direction. What stimuli made certain individuals lean in and retreat. I became adept at using my voice and silence to move the team forward. At the end of my internship, both parties came together and unanimously supported the final direction. The sponsor, my manager, and teammates credited me for being the catalyst. The brand ended up doubling down on a wellness play without alienating their existing audience.

More than the success of the project, I discovered one of the key skills that set me apart in my career. It's reading the room well to know when and how to speak out. Since then, I've often taken the first few days with a team to first observe and learn before jumping in with my thoughts and recommendations.

### Enlisting Others' Feedback Helps You See Your Blindspots.

Getting feedback burns through your ego. It's not easy to receive. However, without feedback, you risk staying blind to your blindspots. Your blindspots are things about you that others can see but you don't. Not knowing these can make you lose out on areas where you can grow and improve. It could also end up posing danger as you make decisions based on an incomplete view of who you are.

To dial up your efficacy in speaking out, regularly check in with others whose opinions you trust are as objective as humanly possible. To get a more rounded view of how others perceive, seek input from varied sources.

These inputs aren't meant to be followed to a T. They serve only as additional information to increase your self-awareness. You need not act on each one of them. You can simply notice that a given perception is how you may be viewed by others.

Not all feedback is critical either. Many times, you are your worst critic. Learning how others view you could enlighten you to bright spots about yourself. The Dove brand once had a campaign called Real Beauty. In it, loved ones were asked to describe the person to a sketcher. The artist then revealed an illustration to the persons described post the interview. Most subjects were pleasantly surprised by what others saw in them. They only picked out all the insecurities while their loved ones mainly focused on the things that made them beautiful.

When speaking out, seek feedback. In this manner, you gain a clearer picture of how you're progressing in developing this skill. You may be pleasantly surprised by how far you've already come while embracing the areas of growth that you still get to work on.

Set a steady and manageable pace that you can keep long term. Remembering that it takes your whole life to master the skill of speaking out for yourself will help you focus on a few battles at a time. This isn't a sprint that you must take on every battle at once. Speaking out is a lifelong marathon. As with any endurance race, give yourself time without rushing. Otherwise, you'll get too overwhelmed and quit prematurely.

To speak out more powerfully, deepen and widen your perspective. You can do this through learning from others. In the next chapter, you'll learn how you can gain more valuable insights that can create a more informed personal worldview that aids in enhancing your self-expression.

# CHAPTER 9

# Grow Your Knowledge to Keep Speaking Out

**ONE HABIT THAT COMPLEMENTS** speaking out is reading good books. You empty your insight vessel by speaking out. You read and experience new things to fill it back up. The more cycles of filling and emptying you go through in a given period, the more opportunities you're giving yourself to deepen and widen your perspectives.

Being knowledgeable or educated isn't a prerequisite for your voice to be worthy. Your voice matters unconditionally. Why then should you engage in lifelong learning as you train yourself to speak out more? Here are the top reasons.

**1. Gain self-awareness and practice self-acceptance.**

The more you imbue your mind with learning, the more you become self-aware. You digest other people's stories or lessons learned and they either alienate you or they strike a chord. The more you see the contrasts and similarities between you and others, the more you learn your preferences and triggers. The more you expose yourself to possibilities and experiment, you find out what comes naturally to you, what's doable, and where you are limited.

As your self-awareness increases, you can then practice self-acceptance. Seeing the various facets of yourself—the good, great, bad, and ugly—is a needed step before you embrace yourself wholly.

Self-acceptance is key to stop hiding your voice and start revealing it. When you focus on who you are instead of who you should be, you experience the freedom of letting what's within you out into the open. You stop getting distracted by what others say about you. You hone in on being true to yourself in thoughts, words, and actions.

As you align your internal and external worlds, you feel at peace. You master your thoughts rather than letting your thoughts master you. You're in control, steering your life as the Queen that you are rather than allowing others to dictate how you live and move around the world.

### 2. Learn many variations of saying what you mean.

When you speak out, you can be at a loss for words. Sometimes, it's not that there are no words to express how you feel. Rather, your command of the language can be further enriched.

The more you read, the more you encounter the

different ways you can express a given thought or feeling. This gives you phrasing templates and samples to dial up your articulation in revealing what's within you. At first, you pattern your wordings based on what you read. Then you create your own style of communicating. Don't let the fear of not being original stop you from getting good at speaking out. Most great and original artists started their journey by first copying others' techniques.

You don't need fancier words. Seeing different phrasing of the same concept can unlock meaning you haven't encountered before. This will help you construct your statements precisely as you mean it.

### 3. See the world with a more nuanced filter.

When you only consume snippets of information as opposed to perusing knowledge, your brain fills in the data gaps with assumptions. These assumptions are based on previously held biases. From this place, you speak out in generalizations. When you do this often, it could dampen your confidence to articulate well. And maintaining confidence is important to keep on speaking out for yourself.

The more you learn, the more you see the world with greater specificity. You gain appreciation of nuances. You stop accepting others' opinions at face value. You dive deeper to determine their significance and accuracy. You become keen and selective of the content you let ruminate in your mind.

Lifelong learning prevents you from being a prey of shallow thinking and fake news. Having a strong knowledge base on a wide range of topics makes you more discerning of articles and opinions you see in your news feeds or hear in conversations. You become less tolerant of unquestioned assumptions and imposed opinions from others. Soon, the need to establish boundaries become more obvious. You gain a greater drive to speak out to keep a distance from trivia that don't serve your healing, growth, and peace.

**4. Learn your position on matters.**

The more you learn, the greater clarity you have on where you stand on moral issues. Going with the flow makes you unanchored. At a glance, it seems like this would be the way toward peaceful relations. However, not knowing where you stand will make you prone to being tossed by whatever the majority or the most powerful believe. In this situation, you're not being a captain of yourself but a yes-woman. Instead, have a stance while staying open, listening to others, and researching. Change your views should new data and interpretation refute old thinking.

You won't know if you have an opinion on a given matter or what your stance is unless that subject is brought up to you. Instead of waiting for circumstances to force you to examine your beliefs, be proactive and expose yourself to available patterns of thought. Critically assess what you learn. Then make up your mind on what you believe.

Urgency drums up pressure. Without some forethought of the principles you hold, you'll be easily maneuvered into another's worldviews and plans. Their way of life will work for you only sometimes, if at all.

**5. Increase your quality of thoughts.**

Good books are treasure mines of insights. The more consistently you read, the greater volume of high-quality information you take in. Like a knife sharpened against a rough surface, your thoughts get refined by testing them against new thoughts or new ways of interpreting concepts you already know about.

When you stop learning after formal schooling is over, your understanding of the world around you is left unchecked. It stays grounded on obsolete concepts. Your thinking dulls. Out of the abundance of your mind, you speak. So if your mind hasn't been renewed, then your speech will reflect it.

To keep evolving your mind, you must continue to expose yourself to and reflect on new ways of seeing and perceiving things. Then you can decide whether to keep your old ways of thinking or refresh them.

**6. Test your assumptions.**

You need not believe everything you learn, no matter how much you like the subject, position, or teacher. Your existing worldview will get challenged. If you press on, you'll either have a more refined outlook or a strengthened conviction of existing beliefs. In this manner, reading good books is like sharpening the axe that is your mind. And your mind is your greatest asset. It's the engine with which you transform your speech.

Changing your mind is valid. It's a sign of growth and progress. If you always think of the same things, then you'll always live in the same way. To change your thinking is to alter the trajectory of your life. When you change your thoughts and words, then your actions, habits, character, and quality of life follow.

You can have a point of view now and have that point change later when you have more data that changes your thoughts. Ideas are fluid.

**7. Gain appreciation for speaking out without knowing all the answers.**

You've observed people talking only to hear themselves. You don't want to be like them because they appear foolish and arrogant. Do you hesitate speaking your mind unless you have a complete grasp of the subject because you fear seeming dumb? The more you read, the more you'll realize that many people speak out effectively without knowing everything. They own their truth and share it not because it is perfect but because many could benefit from their unique views. They share what they know and could know at the moment.

You may be paralyzed by the fear of not knowing how to respond to a rebuttal. When you learn more, you'll begin to see that speaking out doesn't mean you have it all figured out. The more you know, the more you realize you have more to learn. And that awareness makes you more accepting of not knowing everything. This doesn't mean you become careless with your words. Rather, it shuts down the excuse that to speak out, you must know your topic perfectly. You can keep waiting to speak out until you know everything if you're okay waiting a lifetime.

## Why Read Books over Other Learning Forms?

There are many effective ways to engage in lifelong learning—taking courses, listening to podcasts, talking with people, traveling to immerse yourself in a new culture, experimenting, and reading books. Why choose to read books as your most constant form of learning?

**1. Books cause you to think critically and inspire you to introspect.**

When you first pick up a book, you are unbeknownst to the highs, lows, and everything in the middle you will encounter within each chapter. With each flip of a page, your mind registers and processes new bundles of the author's truth. Whether you agree with them or not, you still benefit from the mental exercise that comes with making sense of what you're reading.

Fresh mindsets and beliefs, which may or may not align with what you previously held, swirl and linger in your mind. You have room to sit and reflect with each reading session. There are no forced assessments on whether you did well or not. Will you retain or toss what you learned? How long will you let the thoughts stir and sit with you? You get to play with ideas and choose what to do with them. All the while you're reading, your mind is working—thinking critically and reflecting.

While episodes and articles can drop some truth and insight bombs, it doesn't explore a topic deep enough to stimulate your mind and expand your thinking. As the effort and time investment required is at the lowest with bite-sized content, you tend to be a spectator versus a student. With books, you hold focus longer than what it takes to scroll through a page. This directed energy strengthens your neural circuits. Over time and with consistency, you develop mental resilience while gaining rich perspectives on the topic you are reading about.

## 2. Books elevate your status and quality of life with virtually no restriction.

Books have served many thinkers and doers, strategists and builders, pioneers and purveyors for centuries. They may have evolved in formats over time, as now we have digital copies and audiobooks. Yet they remain in structure as they were originally devised. Books are a condensed and curated learning of a person or a group of people. They reflect their thinking for the time they've thought them. They are distilled information from years of experience. They're the tool of choice for change makers to keep their mind fit because you can, in essence, gain many gems in one reading what the author took years to learn.

You can access virtually any book that has been published at any point in human history. Books aren't exclusive to your place of birth, gender, age, or race. If you have the ability and drive to consistently read and learn, you can digest any book that interests you. This makes books a ticket to uplevel your thinking patterns regardless of your starting point. And as mindsets dictate what you eventually become, books, then, are your lever to enhance your health, status, relationships, and quality of life.

**3. Reading books make it convenient to form a habit of lifelong learning.**

Often, you refuse to learn because you have no time, money, or energy for it. But as with any worthwhile investment, intentionality is a must. And when you're convinced that learning will change how you carry yourself, think, and live your life, you'll make room for it where you once saw no space. You'll reduce time on other activities to make reading possible. When you believe that learning will help you speak out for yourself more confidently, open doors, get you unstuck, and increase your health, you'll do what it takes to make reading a daily priority.

Reading books is a favorable form of learning because it's convenient. You can make it personalized to you. There's no grading, competition, or pressure to outperform anyone. It's you versus you. Are you getting more insightful with each reading, application, and reflection? You determine what success looks like for you.

You can be as flexible with reading as your lifestyle permits. There's no one style, pace, volume, or cadence that fits all. You can read without leaving home, or you can read through audiobooks, while walking your dog, doing errands, or driving. You can read at any time of the day. You can go as fast or as slow as you have interest, energy, and focus.

You have the freedom to start, stop, and restart at any time. As your needs fluctuate, you can pick up what you've parked and park what you've picked up. A book that doesn't work for you now doesn't mean it's useless. It's simply not for you in this season of your life. Be free from the guilt of not finishing a book that doesn't spark or hold your interest. Similarly, there's no shame in re-reading a book you said at one point was ineffective. The beautiful thing about reading a book is you can put it down one moment, pick it back up another time, or finish it in one sitting. You get to decide what's best for you.

You can choose to go fully analog with it. Reading physical books is an experience unlike its digital forms. You can study without distractions and do what author Cal Newport calls "deep work," a concentrated period of studying without interruptions. You get to flow. Your mind comes up with creative insights you've not encountered prior. You won't have blue light disrupting your circadian rhythm and keeping you from having a good sleep. You can write notes, dog-ear pages, or keep a book in pristine condition. It's all up to you.

There's also more than enough books that will last your lifetime of learning. You can access it with one click or choose to wait until you can borrow a physical copy from a library.

### How to Make Book Reading a Daily Habit.

**1. Start with inspiring books.**

You're likely to keep doing what you enjoy doing. You won't need a reminder or external motivation when you like doing something. If you like dancing, a good beat will start your movement with no other push. If you like shopping, no one will need to pay you to do it. You gladly gravitate toward activities you find fun to do. So to make useful tasks stick, it's apt for it to be as enjoyable as possible for you.

When beginning a habit of reading daily, start with inspiring books. It may be tempting to go after the popular but dry nonfiction ones. But if you're yawning after five pages, your brain remembers. The next time you try to crack a book open, your mind will remind you how boring or painful the experience was. Then you'll likely give up reading books altogether. In contrast, if you're left feeling uplifted or empowered after reading, you'll likely keep doing it.

Reserve the drier but helpful books to read later when you have locked in the daily habit of reading books.

**2. Start with tiny books.**

Similarly, a book may be incredibly inspiring but too dense to be your starting point. If you go after the big books with lots of pages, your brain can feel intimidated. Finishing a chapter could feel daunting. You won't believe you can finish an entire book. And if you're not able to visualize a strong finish, the finish will not come.

Going after a tiny book can feel doable. The resistance to read is lowest when the book is least wordy. It may only take you an hour in total to finish it, while reading at a comfortable pace. Of course, reading something short but unhelpful is a waste of time.

Start with tiny and inspiring books with 100 pages or less. A few I recommend are *Man's Search for Meaning* by Viktor Frankl, *Your Next Level Life* by Karen Arrington, and *The Four Agreements* by Don Miguel Ruiz.

**3. Start with ten minutes a day.**

Pull out your calendar now and book ten minutes per day for the next thirty days for reading. Then, show up as you would for any other important appointments. As with businesses that charge a no-show fee, set what your no-show penalty would be. Then, get accountability. Have a friend check on you and charge you your no-show fee.

The impact of reading books is huge when done consistently over time. Physically, you'll be creating new brain cells and strengthening neural circuits. Both are good to keep your brain healthy and ward off memory issues down the line. When your brain is healthy, you remember more, focus better, and think with greater creativity. Psychologically, reading books will make you feel unstuck. When you feel like your life is moving and you're not in a rut, you'll feel more optimistic. Problems remain yet they won't seem final. You're in pain while holding on to hope.

**4. Track your progress.**

What gets measured gets done. Whether it's a check mark on the calendar or an app that tracks your reading streak, measure your progress. When you do, you become aware of how many days you've completed or missed your ten-minute reading sessions. This awareness is powerful. It forces you to face your reality than tuck it away. Notice your pattern without self-shaming. See this as data to inform you on what to optimize in your reading system. You may do better reading early in the morning versus before bed or the reverse. You may notice that mixing in audiobooks allows you to stick to your habit versus purely reading physical books. You may find that posting about what you read on social media keeps you accountable. Or you may discover that keeping your reading private takes the pressure off so you do it more frequently. Tracking is key to be attuned to what works, what doesn't, what's good to keep doing, and what needs changing.

**5. Celebrate when you finish.**

Create mini-milestones to keep your reading going. What small thing will you give yourself as a reward for completing seven ten-minute sessions? What will you get when you hit that halfway mark in reading a book? You can give yourself the reward of getting your next book or a cup of your favorite drink. Incentives can create enthusiasm as you begin creating a practice. Once you've made reading a lifestyle, you won't be needing them as often.

Speaking out feels intimidating. It's even more terrifying when you feel like you don't have substantial ideas to share. Increase your confidence in speaking out through increasing your wealth of knowledge. Book reading is an effective form of daily learning.

# CONCLUSION
## Let's Hear You Roar, Queen

**THE VOICE WITHIN YOU** that you thought had died is alive. It's only buried underneath layers of social conditioning, trauma, and deceit. And you alone can resuscitate it. You have what it takes to be all you are meant to be. Now, you also carry the tools to wake up your drowned-out truth.

You're in your season of voice redemption.

Embody the mindset of tenacity, curiosity, and self-compassion to bring forth the hidden gems within you. You are worthy of a life of meaning and authenticity.

You need not dim your brilliance and keep silent to make others feel comfortable around you. Comfort is okay if experienced sparingly. Chronic comfort, though, does more damage than good.

For your self-healing, speaking out is a necessity. Without it, depression, broken relationships, eating disorders, addiction, irritable bowel syndrome, and a life less than what's available for you fester.

Self-care isn't selfish. It's your core. You can give more from a place of health and overflow than sickness and drought.

Having a voice is a practice. This means it won't be a one-time occurrence. It's not supposed to be perfect. What's key is that you show up and keep honing this life skill.

Remember, the people who root for you are seeking you too. Find your tribe to help you go further. There is power in community, especially in the community of empowered Queens.

Know that you're in the driver seat on this journey. Speak out how you want to, when you want to, and in what situations you want to. Release the pressure of speaking out as others do. Be unique in your self-expression and selective about who you surround yourself with.

Read good books daily. Fill up on knowledge, insights, and inspiration.

A life you love is on the other side of you speaking out for yourself, Queen. And you're worthy, equipped, and emboldened to take a seat on the throne of your life.

Now, show yourself who you are and what you're capable of becoming. You're entitled as a human being to get to know and live out the real you.

Be.

# Acknowledgments

To my constant, Abba, Jesus, and Holy Spirit, thank You for choosing me to carry this gift. All glory is Yours.

To my husband, Mike, thank you for your love, loyalty, and support, even when it's not always easy or convenient.

To my family. Mom (RIP) and Dad, for raising me to know and believe in myself, you are my heroes. My younger siblings Micah, Lauriz, and Renz, thank you for having my back no matter what. My soul and spirit sister, Fatimah, for sharing this journey with me. My Hortillosa and Sandoval family, thank you for cheering me on and praying for me. My friends and extended family, thank you for your encouragement.

To my editor, Jenna Love-Schrader, my book cover designer, Matt Davies, and my typesetter, Laura Jones, you're good at what you do, easy to work with, and professional at all times. Thank you for polishing this book to its final form.

To the following people for their inspiration: J&J and P&G former mentors and colleagues, Karen Arrington,

Monica Lewinsky, Sara Dahan, James Altucher, James Clear, and Julian Treasure.

To my offline and online community, coaching clients, and Cocoon Coffee family, you give me purpose. Thank you for showing up for me and each other.

# About the Author

**Christine H. Sandoval** is a writer, coach, and entrepreneur, helping finishers in transition rebuild their self-worth after an exit.

Previously, she was a corporate leader at Johnson & Johnson and Procter & Gamble.

She received her Doctorate of Pharmacy from the University of Texas at Austin in 2013 and her Master of Business Administration from Xavier University in 2016. She currently lives in Austin, Texas, with her husband Mike and dog Asher.

More info about Christine's work can be found at drchristinesandoval.com.

# Book Review

Was this book helpful to you in some way? If so, I'd love to learn about it. Honest reviews help readers find the right book for their needs.

Made in the USA
Las Vegas, NV
24 July 2022

52104959R00100